Supporting Grade 5–8 Students in Constructing Explanations in Science

Supporting Grade 5–8 Students in Constructing Explanations in Science

The Claim, Evidence, and Reasoning Framework for Talk and Writing

Katherine L. McNeill

Boston College

Joseph J. Krajcik

University of Michigan

Boston   Columbus   Indianapolis   New York   San Francisco   Upper Saddle River
Amsterdam   Cape Town   Dubai   London   Madrid   Milan   Munich   Paris   Montreal   Toronto
Delhi   Mexico City   Sao Paulo   Sydney   Hong Kong   Seoul   Singapore   Taipei   Tokyo

Senior Editor: Kelly Villella Canton
Editorial Assistant: Annalea Manalili
Vice President, Director of Marketing: Maggie Waples
Marketing Manager: Danae April
Production Editor: Karen Mason
Editorial Production Service and Electronic Composition: TexTech International
Manufacturing Buyer: Megan Cochran
Photo Researcher: Annie Pickert

Credits and acknowledgments borrowed from other sources and reproduced, with permission, in this textbook appear on appropriate page within text.

Photo Credits: Zuma Wire West/Newscom, pp. 1, 18; Frances M. Roberts/Newscom, p. 43; Mike Gould, Photographer, cover and pp. 66, 94; Shutterstock, p. 80; Paul Sancya/AP, p. 122; Odessa American/AP, p. 143.

This material is based on work supported by the National Science Foundation ("NSF") under Grant No. DRL-0836099. Any opinions, findings, and conclusions or recommendations expressed in this material are those of the author(s) and do not necessarily reflect the views of the National Science Foundation.

Library of Congress Cataloging-in-Publication Data

McNeill, Katherine L.
    Supporting grade 5–8 students in constructing explanations in science : the claim, evidence, and reasoning framework for talk and writing / Katherine L. McNeill, Joseph Krajcik.
        p. cm.
    Includes bibliographical references and index.
    ISBN-10: 0-13-704345-7
    ISBN-13: 978-0-13-704345-3
    1. Science—Study and teaching (Middle school)   I. Krajcik, Joseph S.   II. Title.
    LB1585.M38 2012
    372.35—dc22

                                                                2010039996

9 2021

www.pearsonhighered.com

ISBN-10:   0-13-704345-7
ISBN-13: 978-0-13-704345-3

We dedicate this book to all the teachers with whom we worked for *their* dedication to improving the lives of the children they teach. We also dedicate this book to our spouses, Ryan and Ann, for their continuous encouragement, consistent support, and love.

Contents

Contents for Video Clips

Foreword

As the Director of Science in Boston, I am reminded every day that there are children who would be "left behind" if not for the hard work and dedication of the teachers who take them from where they are to where they need to be. Many students have not had the opportunity to learn what they need to become strong readers, good writers, and inquiring scientists. The emphasis in many of our schools has been on state test scores, AYP, and staying off the list of failing schools—this translates to more time on ELA and math—and not enough time on science. This year, passing the statewide science exam has become high stakes for us—if children don't pass, they don't graduate. One would think that this would get people's attention—lending credibility to my claim that we need science taught to every child, everyday.

To me, science levels the playing field; children who have not yet found success in school can be successful doing science. All children come to school with a natural curiosity and if we are careful and teach science effectively, we can help students see science as a way of knowing the world around them. We could use science instructional time to strengthen students' literacy skills as well. There is so much ground to "uncover," that we must cross boundaries and target high yield strategies—those with the greatest potential to support students as they learn science and develop their literacy skills. Scientific explanation—using claim, evidence and reasoning as a framework for thinking in science—is one way for students to dialogue about their developing understandings and provides a structure for writing that represents science inquiry effectively.

In our district, Kate McNeill and Joe Krajcik's Claim, Evidence and Reasoning (CER) work has been at the core of our efforts in science, not only at the middle school, but at the elementary and high school levels as well. Last year, I was asked to co-lead a "writing across the content areas" initiative, the Common Writing Assignment. I knew early on that I wanted our work to focus on students' explanation and argumentation in science; I also knew that I needed help! All students in grades 4–8 (and now we have expanded to high school) were asked to respond to a prompt by making a claim, providing evidence from their classroom and laboratory experiences, and linking the claim and evidence with scientific reasoning. A colleague recommended that I have a conversation with Kate. We utilized the CER work to develop writing prompts and design our rubric. The

CER framework has been woven into the fabric of science instruction—not only is it a guide for discourse and writing, but it is fast becoming part of the culture of teaching and learning science in our district.

Our teachers are excited about using the CER framework and have embraced this work. Using this book as part of teacher professional development has been transforming teacher practice. They tell me over and over about how they love the way this "comes together" for them. Kate and Joe's strategies for integrating scientific explanation are efficient and effective. I have seen improvement in the quality of science talk and writing taking place in our classrooms. Students' understanding of what science is and what it does is strengthened by this emphasis on scientific explanation and argumentation. Through *Supporting Grade 5-8 Students in Constructing Scientific Explanations*, Kate and Joe have provided a tool for our teachers to more effectively challenge and support our students and for this, I am grateful.

Pam Pelletier
Senior Program Director for Science, K-12
Boston Public Schools
Boston, Massachusetts

Preface

Helping all children learn about the natural world and engage in scientific inquiry practices are the primary goals of science education in schools today. In *Supporting Grade 5–8 Students in Constructing Explanations in Science: The Claim, Evidence, and Reasoning Framework for Talk and Writing,* we focus on how to support students in constructing scientific explanations to achieve both goals. Because the work of scientists involves explaining how and why phenomena occur and debating alternative explanations with other scientists, scientific explanation is an essential component of the field of science and should also be an important part of the teaching of science. In order to be proficient, students need to be able to generate scientific evidence, explain natural phenomena, and participate in science talk and science writing (Michaels, Shouse, & Schweingruber, 2008). In this book, we show you how to engage your students in this essential work of scientists.

In addition to emulating what scientists do, there are multiple benefits for students who construct scientific explanations. Our research has shown that engaging middle grade students in scientific explanation analysis and writing positively impacts students' ability to use evidence, to justify their claims, and to engage in scientific reasoning (Krajcik, McNeill, & Reiser, 2008; McNeill, Lizotte, Krajcik, & Marx, 2006; McNeill & Krajcik, 2009). Furthermore, constructing scientific explanations supports students in learning important core science ideas and concepts (Bell & Linn, 2000; Krajcik et al., 2008; McNeill et al., 2006; McNeill & Krajcik, 2009; Zohar & Nemet, 2002). Students also learn essential twenty-first-century skills such as communication, critical thinking, complex problem solving, and adaptive learning strategies that are all believed to contribute to career readiness and workforce success (Krajcik & Sutherland, 2009). So it is important that every student know how to construct scientific explanations.

The role of teachers and how they use the different instructional strategies discussed in this book are essential to improving students' content understanding and increasing students' abilities to construct scientific explanations (McNeill & Krajcik, 2008a; McNeill & Krajcik, 2009; McNeill, 2009). The strategies and scaffolds that we present will help you support all students, including English language learners (ELLs) and students with special needs, develop proficiency with this important scientific practice. We present a framework that we have used for

10 years and that has subsequently been used by numerous teachers to guide and support students to develop greater competence and expertise with this challenging practice. The framework for scientific explanation (McNeill et al., 2006) consists of making a *claim* and of using *evidence* and *reasoning* to support the claim. As students advance in their ability to engage in this scientific practice, we then introduce the idea of a *rebuttal*. The framework and instructional strategies we discuss build on national science education standards, such as *The Benchmarks for Science Literacy* (AAAS, 1993) and *National Science Education Standards* (NRC, 1996), as well as recent reform documents in science education, such as *Taking Science to School* (Duschl, Schweingruber, & Shouse, 2007) and *Ready, Set, Science!* (Michaels et al., 2008).

Engaging students in constructing scientific explanation represents a fundamental shift in how to teach science. Although numerous teachers have used the scientific explanation framework successfully in their classrooms, this model may be quite different from the way you have taught science in the past. You will be called on to develop new teaching strategies, including more open-ended questioning, an emphasis on using evidence, and more facilitation of discussions in which students debate their position with reasoning and evidence. We hope that our book and the explanation framework it describes encourage you to teach science in new ways that successfully engage all your students in the fundamental aspects of science.

Scientific Explanation Framework

- **Claim**—A statement or conclusion that answers the original question/problem.
- **Evidence**—Scientific data that supports the claim.
- **Reasoning**—A justification that connects the evidence to the claim using scientific principles.
- **Rebuttal**—Recognizes and describes alternative explanations, and provides counter evidence and reasoning for why the alternative explanation is not appropriate.

Overview of the Chapters

Chapter 1 provides a justification for why students should construct scientific explanations, presents a classroom example of students constructing scientific explanations, and describes the challenges students face in both their writing and their classroom discussions. In Chapter 2, we introduce the scientific explanation framework of claim, evidence, reasoning, and rebuttal as well as provide examples of student writing and a video to illustrate how to introduce the framework to your students. Chapter 3 focuses on planning and designing your classroom instruction to support students in constructing scientific explanations. We first discuss how you can identify places that are optimal for using the scientific explanation framework in your current curriculum. We then examine how to design and create learning tasks with varying degrees of complexity so that students with a range of experiences and background knowledge can take part in this practice. Finally, we discuss how you can develop classroom supports, such as curricular scaffolds and visual representations, to aid students in the practice. In Chapter 4, we discuss several essential teaching strategies (and video examples of teachers implementing them in a range of grade 5–8 classrooms) to guide your students with scientific explanation construction.

After discussing how to integrate the scientific explanation framework in your classroom, we then shift to developing assessments and providing students with support over time. Chapter 5 takes you through a systematic process of designing assessment items and the associated rubrics for scientific explanations. Several examples will illustrate what the steps look like in practice. One major focus of the chapter is on creating assessment items that align with the learning goals of both the science content and scientific explanations. In Chapter 6, we explore how you can use rubrics to analyze student work to uncover the students' strengths and weaknesses as well as to inform your own instruction. The chapter provides and discusses several examples of student writing in order to illustrate this process. Finally, in Chapter 7, we explore how to support student learning over time. We discuss how the framework can be used to change the conversation in your classroom to foster a shift from a more teacher-focused to a more student-focused classroom culture in which students share and debate ideas among themselves. Additionally, you will learn how to work with your colleagues across grades to introduce more sophisticated notions of the scientific explanation framework over time and how the framework can be connected to other content areas such as mathematics, English language arts, and social studies to support a school culture that prioritizes the use of evidence and reasoning to justify claims.

Key Features of the Book

- First, each chapter starts with a *vignette* (or scenario) that provides a vision of what using scientific explanations looks like in a grade 5–8 teacher's science classroom. These vignettes focus on the core ideas discussed in each chapter in order to illustrate what those ideas will look like in classroom practice.
- Second, we incorporate numerous examples of *students' written work* throughout the book to show you what students at various grade levels with different background knowledge and experience can accomplish. These examples also illustrate common student difficulties with constructing scientific explanations and strategies for supporting those challenges.
- Third, we include *video clips* to help you see how other teachers introduce and support scientific explanations in their classrooms. These video clips illustrate the different strategies as well as come from a range of grade levels and contexts to demonstrate what the use of the scientific explanation framework can look like in actual classrooms.

- Fourth, we provide *strategies to support all students* in learning how to take part and succeed in this practice, including English language learners and students with special needs. These strategies are often summarized in tables and include classroom examples to illustrate the strategies in practice.
- Fifth, we include a *check point* to provide a summary of the ideas discussed in each chapter as well as provide an overview of the concepts to be discussed in future chapters. These check points provide a road map for the progression of ideas discussed throughout the book.
- Lastly, each chapter ends with *study group questions* that help you construct meaning and apply what you read in the chapter to your own work with students. You may want to answer or discuss these questions with fellow teachers who are also reading the book and integrating scientific explanations into their own classrooms.

Our goal is to present and illustrate the lessons we have learned by working with teachers in classrooms to provide you with strategies to support your students in this important, yet difficult, task of constructing scientific explanations. Your students will grow up in a world in which they will need to be able to support claims with evidence and evaluate the arguments and claims of others. We hope that *Supporting Grade 5–8 Students in Constructing Explanations in Science: The Claim, Evidence, and Reasoning Framework for Talk and Writing* will help you integrate scientific explanations throughout your teaching to change the way students learn science and support students in the development of core science ideas and important twenty-first-century skills.

Acknowledgments

This book would not have been possible without the inspiration and dedication of our colleagues to improve the teaching and learning of science for all children. We would like to thank the many science teachers we have worked with who gave us ideas to further our own thinking about how to enact scientific explanations in the classroom. We are particularly grateful to the teachers in this book who let us into their classroom to videotape their interactions. Without their courage and agreement to share the videos, we would have a different product. In particular, we would like to thank Dean Martin from Gardner Pilot Academy in Boston, MA, and Ann Novak from Greenhills School in Ann Arbor, MI not only for inviting us into their classrooms, but also for their valuable feedback in reviewing the initial draft of the book. We also acknowledge the contributions of our higher education colleagues in hice at the University of Michigan—LeeAnn Sutherland, Elizabeth Moje, Charles Dershimer, and Ronald Marx (now at the University of Arizona)—and those at Northwestern University—Brian Reiser and Leema Berland (now at University of Texas at Austin) who helped us first develop these ideas. We would like to thank Gerhard Salinger, from the National Science Foundation, whose vision for improving science education not only provided essential feedback and support for this work but has helped to foster more widespread changes in science education. Furthermore, the teachers, science supervisors and teacher educators who reviewed this book offered insightful comments to improve the clarity of our writing. These reviewers are Barbara A. Bedford Johnson, Pioneer Middle School; Pete DeRiso, North Warren Regional School District; Kelly M. Graveson, Douglas High School; Bruce Kamerer, Donald McKay K-8 School; Suzanna Loper, University of California, Berkeley, Lawrence Hall of Science; Jennifer Lowary, Arvada Middle School; Erin McNally, Trevor Day School; Alycia Meriweather, Detroit Public Schools, Detroit Mathematics and Science Center; Pam Pelletier, Boston Public Schools; Lee Ann Nickerson, Jefferson County Public Schools; Kendra Walters Durham, Wester Middle School; and Carla Zembal-Saul, The Pennsylvania State University. Finally, we would like to thank Kelly Villella Canton, our editor, who not only sought us out and encouraged us to write this book, but who also provided excellent guidance and editing when we accepted her offer.

About the Authors

Katherine L. McNeill is an assistant professor of science education at Boston College. A former middle school science teacher, she received her doctorate in science education from the University of Michigan. Her research focuses on helping students with diverse backgrounds become interested in science and learn both science content and scientific inquiry practices. Specifically, she has recently focused on how to support students in engaging in scientific explanation and argumentation in both talk and writing. Her research has been generously funded by the National Science Foundation (NSF). She has published numerous book chapters and journal articles from her research, including articles in the *Journal of Research in Science Teaching, Science Education,* the *Journal of the Learning Sciences,* and the *International Journal of Science Education.* She has also conducted numerous workshops at the annual meeting of the National Teachers Association (NSTA) and for school districts including the Detroit Public Schools and the Boston Public Schools.

Joseph Krajcik, a professor at the University of Michigan, develops classroom environments in which students find solutions to important intellectual questions that subsume essential learning goals. He is a fellow of the American Association for the Advancement of Science (AAAS) and the American Educational Research Association (AERA), has served as president of the National Associate for Research in Science Teaching (NARST) in 1999, and received guest professorships from Beijing Normal University and the Weizmann Institute of Science. In 2009, he was named a distinguished professor at Ewha Woman's University in South Korea and served as a faculty member at the Institute for Global Science, Technology, and Society Education. In 2010, he received the Distinguished Contributions to Science Education Through Research Award from NARST. Joe is currently serving as co-editor for the Journal of Research in Science Teaching. He has also frequently made presentations for teachers at conferences and workshops in which he translates his empirical work into important lessons for classroom practice.

Importance of Supporting Students in Scientific Explanation

What are the essential components of science? What do these key aspects of science look like in grade 5–8 science classrooms? In order to begin to explore these questions, let's consider the following vignette from Ms. Nelson's seventh-grade classroom.

In the spring, Ms. Nelson's seventh-grade class begins an earth science unit in which they explore the question: What is the water quality of our stream? To answer this question, the students collect several water quality measurements from a stream behind their school. Ms. Nelson assigns groups of students to collect and analyze data from different sections of the stream. Group B, which consists of Cesar, Jennifer, and Josh, collects the following data at site four of the stream during three different times of the month.

Test	Trial 1	Trial 2	Trial 3
pH	7.9	8.2	7.9
Temp Change (°C)	1.8	1.6	1.7
Conductivity (mg/l)	350	293	325
Dissolved Oxygen (%)	64	63	58

Once the students collect the data, Ms. Nelson gives them national standards for water quality and asks each group to use their data and the standards to construct a scientific explanation that answers their research question about the water quality of the stream. The first step students in Group B decide to do is to calculate the average result of each test and add another column to their table to include these averages. Their new data table looks like this:

Test	Trial 1	Trial 2	Trial 3	Average
pH	7.9	8.2	7.9	8.0
Temp Change (°C)	1.8	1.6	1.7	1.7
Conductivity (mg/l)	350	293	325	323
Dissolved Oxygen (%)	64	63	58	62

Next, Group B discusses their results and tries to use their data to determine the water quality of the stream.

> Jennifer: The water quality is good because the pH is in the good range.

> Josh: I disagree. Look—the water quality is only fair because of the conductivity results.

> Cesar: I think the different tests may suggest different things in terms of the water quality. Let's add a column next to the average column that shows how our findings compare to the national standards.

Jennifer and Josh agree with Cesar's suggestion and they add one more column to their table that compares their averages to the national water quality standards.

Test	Trial 1	Trial 2	Trial 3	Average	National Water Standards
pH	7.9	8.2	7.9	8.0	good
Temp Change (°C)	1.8	1.6	1.7	1.7	excellent
Conductivity (mg/l)	350	293	325	323	fair
Dissolved Oxygen (%)	64	63	58	62	fair

Josh: See—the water quality is only fair because both the conductivity and dissolved oxygen are fair.

Cesar: I don't know. What about pH? What about the temperature change?

The three students begin to debate whether the evidence suggests that the water quality is fair or good using their understanding of water quality and the national standards. Later, during a full-class discussion, Group B shares their disagreement with the entire class. They end up using the additional data from the other groups to resolve their debate in order to have sufficient evidence to determine the water quality of the stream.

This vignette shows students engaging in important aspects of what it means to do science in that they are analyzing data, making sense of data, and constructing explanations. The scenario shows students discussing what their stream data means in terms of the water quality and using that data as evidence to support claims that they make to explain real-world phenomena. As such, these students are using and developing important twenty-first-century skills that they will be able to use throughout their lives in a variety of different contexts (National Research Council, 2008).

How can you incorporate similar scientific practices into your classroom? How can you help students develop skills they will need throughout their lives? This book will support you in answering these questions and provide you with strategies to help your students construct scientific explanations. This chapter discusses the role of explanations in science, presents a classroom example of students constructing scientific explanations, provides a justification for why students should construct scientific explanations, and describes the challenges students face in both their writing and during classroom discussions.

The Role of Explanations in Science

Science is fundamentally about explaining the world around us. Scientists try to understand how and why different phenomena occur. For example, they investigate the following kinds of questions: Why is global climate change occurring? Can genetically modified foods be bad for our health? and How can we develop more efficient automobiles? In answering these questions, scientists collect data, make sense of the data and use the data as evidence to explain these complex and important phenomena. The use of evidence drives scientists' understandings of the world around them. For example, to determine the cause for global climate change, scientists often debate whether the changes result from naturally occurring climatic cycles or from human actions. In order to test these different claims, scientists collect data and develop theories for why the evidence supports or refutes the varying claims. Specifically for climate change, scientists analyze data and look for trends in data for air and ocean temperatures, the amount and severity of hurricanes, and the amount of greenhouse gases in the atmosphere. Scientists develop competing claims and debate the validity of those claims with other scientists.

This fundamental practice of developing and critiquing scientific explanations is essential not only for scientists, but also for your students (NRC, 2000 NRC, 2008). When students develop and critique explanations it not only helps them learn the science content, but it can also motivate them to want to study science as they realize learning science is more than just memorizing facts. Furthermore, it prepares them to be scientifically literate adults as they learn to read critically the claims of others and to communicate their own ideas with supporting evidence and reasoning. Students need to engage in this important inquiry practice as they conduct their own explorations of the world around them as well as in science class. For example, fifth-grade students may conduct an investigation about the biodiversity in their schoolyard in order to construct an explanation about why some species are able to survive in that environment. Eighth-grade students may build a Rube Goldberg machine in order to construct an explanation about how energy transfers from one form to another. Inquiry science is not only about engaging students in conducting investigations—it also involves students making sense of those investigations through the process of constructing explanations. The depth of students' ability to learn science depends on this meaning making process.

Scientific Explanations in the Classroom

Our initial interest in scientific explanations stemmed from working with middle school science teachers in a large urban school district. At the time, we were piloting a middle school science curriculum, *How can I make new stuff from old stuff?* (McNeill, Harris, Heitzman, Lizzotte, Sutherland, & Krajcik, 2004), and we were interested in the effectiveness of the science lessons and investigations. The eight-week chemistry unit focused on three key science concepts: substances and properties, chemical reactions and conservation of mass. From observing different lessons, analyzing student writing and talking with teachers it became clear that one challenge across all the science investigations was students' ability to make sense of data and construct scientific explanations in which they justified their claims. Students were engaged in the investigations, but it was this meaning-making piece after the investigations that was challenging.

For example, during the curriculum students collected data on two unknowns (fat and soap) to find out whether they were the same or different substances. Their data collection included color, melting point, solubility, density, and hardness for both substances. Table 1.1 illustrates the data the students collected for fat and soap.

After collecting the data, students then wrote a scientific explanation to answer the following writing prompt: *Write a scientific explanation stating whether fat and*

TABLE 1.1 Student Data Collection for Fat and Soap

			Data		
	Color	Hardness	Solubility	Melting Point	Density
Fat	Off-white or slightly yellow	Soft-squishy	Water—no Oil—yes	~37° C	0.92 g/cm³
Soap	Milky white	Hard	Water—yes Oil—no	Higher than 100° C	0.84 g/cm

soap are the same substance or different substances. Figure 1.1 includes the writing sample for one seventh-grade student, Brandon.[1] This is Brandon's initial scientific explanation about soap and fat being different substances.

Brandon's claim is correct that "fat and soap are both stuff, but they are different substances." Yet he provides little scientific support to justify his claim; instead, he talks about cooking and washing, the purposes of the two substances. Initially, we were surprised that students, like Brandon, did not use the data they had collected in their investigations to support their claims. We soon found that this was a trend in the science writing of upper elementary and middle school students. In

FIGURE 1.1

Brandon's First Explanation about Soap and Fat

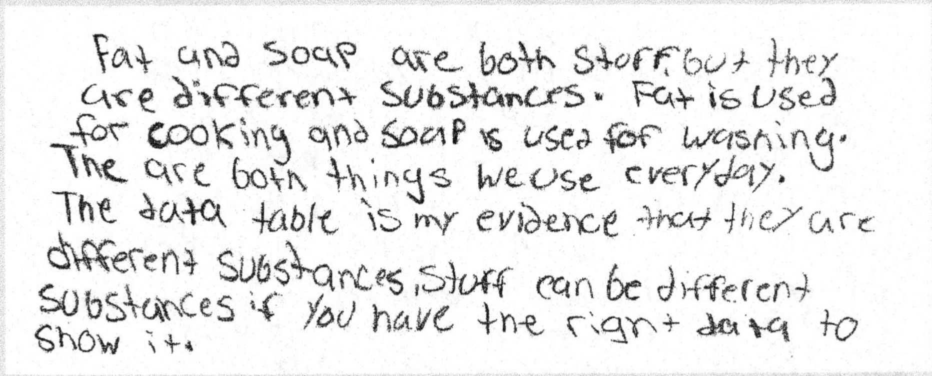

Fat and soap are both stuff, but they are different substances. Fat is used for cooking and soap is used for washing. The are both things we use everyday. The data table is my evidence that they are different substances. Stuff can be different substances if you have the right data to show it.

---

[1]All students' and teachers' names are pseudonyms.

Brandon's case, although his everyday knowledge is important and should be incorporated into the classroom discussion, he also needs to understand that the *purpose* of two objects actually does not tell you if they are *made* of the same substance. For example, both a soda can and an automobile might be made out of aluminum. Although they are made out of the same substance, they have very different purposes. Furthermore, Brandon just states that the data table is his evidence instead of talking about specific information in the data table, such as solubility and density. We found this to be another trend with students. In order to justify his claim, Brandon needs to explicitly provide the evidence and describe why those properties are evidence that fat and soap are different substances.

After the students wrote their initial explanations, their teacher, Mr. Kaplan, conducted a lesson specifically focused on scientific explanation introducing a framework for writing scientific explanation (discussed in Chapter 2) and incorporating various teaching strategies such as modeling examples and providing feedback (discussed in Chapter 4). The framework and teaching strategies came from research we conducted with teachers during the previous two years to help students with scientific explanations (McNeill & Krajcik, 2008a). Mr. Kaplan then asked his students to revise their scientific explanations. Figure 1.2 includes Brandon's revised explanation after the lesson focused on scientific explanations.

FIGURE 1.2
Brandon's Revised Explanation about Soap and Fat

Fat and soap are different substances. Fat is of white and soap is milky white. Fat is soft squishy and soap is hard. Fat is soluble in oil, but soap is not soluble in oil. Soap is soluble in water, but fat is not. Fat has a melting point of 97°C and soap has a melting point above 100°C. Fat has a density of 0.92 g/cm³ and soap has a density of 0.84 g/cm³. These are all properties. Because fat and soap have different properties, I know they are different.

Brandon's revised explanation provides a much stronger justification for his claim that fat and soap are different substances. This example illustrates our goal for students in terms of both their writing and discussions in class. Brandon uses the scientific evidence that he collected in class—color, hardness, solubility, melting point and density. He specifically talks about the evidence and how the characteristics were different for fat and soap. Finally, he describes his reasoning for why this evidence supports his claim: "These are all properties. Because fat and soap have different properties, I know they are different." In just one lesson, Brandon shows impressive improvement in his science writing.

Many of the other students in Mr. Kaplan's class still struggled with justifying their claims after one lesson. Throughout the school year, Mr. Kaplan continued to have students write scientific explanations and used various teaching strategies to support them in this writing. Having students create written responses like this does not happen overnight. Engaging students in constructing strong scientific explanations, like learning anything new, takes careful support and nurturing from teachers. Helping students to articulate and explain their ideas using evidence as exemplified by Brandon's revised explanation presents challenging work for teachers, particularly when students have not been encouraged to use evidence to support their claims in previous science classes. But all students can construct strong scientific explanations when they are provided with sufficient time, practice, and instructional support.

Benefits of Scientific Explanations

Scientific explanations can play a key role in science classrooms offering numerous benefits to teachers and students. The National Research Council released an important report, *Taking Science to School* (Duschl, Schweingruber, & Shouse, 2007), which synthesizes the latest educational research for K-8 science teaching. *Ready, Set Science* (Michaels, Shouse, & Schweingruber, 2008) is a follow-up to the report for science educational practitioners that applies the findings to classroom practice. Both reports advocate four major goals for K-8 students in science: (1) know and use scientific ideas, (2) generate and evaluate scientific evidence and explanations, (3) understand the nature and development of scientific knowledge, and (4) participate productively in scientific practices and discourse. While scientific explanation aligns explicitly with the second goal, the practice of engaging students in scientific explanations can help you achieve all four goals with your students as they participate in these essential aspects of science.

Engaging your students in scientific explanations can provide numerous benefits (McNeill, 2009; McNeill & Krajcik, 2008a; McNeill et al., 2006) such as help them: (1) understand science concepts, (2) develop twenty-first-century skills, (3) use evidence to support claims, (4) reason logically, (5) consider and critique alternative explanations, and (6) understand the nature of science. Improvement in these

why construct scientific explanations?

different areas not only helps them succeed in school science, but also better prepares them to be scientifically literate adults. Furthermore, engaging your students in scientific explanations provides you insight into student thinking, offers excellent assessment opportunities, and provides literacy connections for writing across the content areas. In this section, each of these benefits are discussed in more detail.

Understand Science Concepts

7th grade reaction times → observations on their data → apply scientific ideas to ques "will react improve w/ ____?"

When writing scientific explanations, students apply scientific ideas to answer a question or problem using appropriate evidence. As recommended in *Ready, Set, Science!* (Michaels, Shouse & Schweingruber, 2008), students need to be able to know, use and interpret scientific ideas. Science instruction often involves students conducting investigations or making observations of the world around them. Yet making sense of those experiences and understanding the science concepts involved in those instructional tasks can be challenging for students. Asking students to construct a scientific explanation at the end of an investigation supports students in making sense of their data through the application of science concepts. This assignment can enrich their understanding of the science concepts by helping them make connections and apply the concepts within a new context. Creating a scientific explanation requires students to really think and reason about a phenomenon. For example, in Brandon's writing he had to apply his understanding of substances and properties to determine that fat and soap were different substances. Revising his scientific explanation encouraged him to reflect on and articulate the scientific principles that he was using to answer the question. In the vignette at the beginning of the chapter, during Jennifer, Josh, and Cesar's discussion, they had to apply their understanding of water quality to make sense of the data they had collected from the stream. The act of constructing a scientific explanation requires that students apply concepts in new and flexible ways to make sense of complex scientific phenomena.

Develop Twenty-First-Century Skills

Engaging in scientific explanations also supports students in developing important twenty-first-century skills that are essential for a world being transformed by technology, communication and the growth of knowledge (Rhoton & Shane, 2006). Recently, the National Academies (NRC, 2008) sponsored a report to explore the intersection between science education and the development of twenty-first-century skills. The National Academies identified five broad skills that are essential for a range of twenty-first-century jobs, from low-wage service jobs to professional occupations: (1) adaptability—ability to cope with uncertain and new situations, (2) complex communication—skills in processing, interpreting, and communicating information, (3) nonroutine problem solving—analyzing information, recognizing patterns, and generating solutions, (4) self-management—ability to be self-motivating and self-monitoring and (5) systems thinking—systems analysis, systems evaluation, and adopting a big picture perspective. Incorporating scientific explanation in your classroom can support your students in acquiring the first four of these skills (Krajcik & Sutherland, 2009). Since scientific explanation can be adapted across a variety of content, it can help students adapt to new situations, communicate with others, engage in problem solving, and support them in their own self-monitoring.

Use of Evidence to Support Claims

Another recommendation of *Ready, Set, Science!* (2008) is to generate and use evidence, which the authors discuss as being at the heart of science. We agree that using evidence is essential to science. Unfortunately, in science classrooms students often do not make use of evidence they collect. Conducting investigations can become more procedural and less focused on the use of evidence to answer a question or explain phenomena. Using evidence is critically important to communicate convincingly to other people. Being able to write in this particular way can help students in future learning and in real world contexts as it provides them with an excellent opportunity to practice two twenty-first-century skills—complex communication and nonroutine problem solving. For example, evidence is often used in nonscientific fields, as in the media and popular culture to support claims such as why you should buy a particular product, vote for a particular politician or support the building of a new school in town. Individuals need to be critical of that evidence in examining whether the evidence is appropriate for the claim and whether there is enough evidence to support the claim as they make decisions in their everyday lives.

Reason Logically

Engaging in scientific explanations often improves students' ability to reason in science as they become more adept at this type of analytical thinking. In many science classrooms, we have noticed not only a change in students' writing, but also a change in classroom discussions. For example, in one seventh-grade classroom a student proposed that making Kool-Aid was a chemical reaction. The teacher probed the student by asking for her evidence to support that claim, which initiated a classroom debate about how you could determine whether or not making Kool-Aid is a chemical reaction. One student said that his evidence was that the Kool-Aid tasted different after you mixed it. Other students in the class disagreed, stating that taste was not evidence of a chemical reaction; rather, they needed to examine properties such as color and density to determine if they had really made a new substance. This type of questioning and reasoning is essential in science not only for scientists, but also for all scientifically literate citizens. Questioning is critical to fostering an inquiry orientation in your classroom. Scientific explanations highlight the role of using reasoning to show why the data are evidence for the claim and applying scientific principles to understand phenomena. Students need encouragement and support to engage in this type of logical reasoning whenever they are making sense of their science experiences.

Consider and Critique Alternative Explanations

Having students construct their own scientific explanations also encourages them to grow more constructively critical of other individuals' spoken and written explanations. Engaging in scientific explanations requires students to consider how other people are justifying their claims and whether or not their justifications are appropriate. Knowing how to listen to the evidence and justifications provided by others is an important component of being able to communicate. Furthermore, students need to be able to construct rebuttals where they defend why an alternative explanation is not appropriate for a particular question. For example, in the water quality vignette from Ms. Nelson's class the students debated alternative explanations of their stream data trying to determine whether the water quality was fair or good. This type of critical stance helps people better assess science topics not only in science class, but also when presented in popular culture. Controversial science issues, such as cloning, nuclear energy, or global climate change, crop up frequently in magazines, on television, and on the Internet. For people to be critical consumers of popular science who make informed decisions in their everyday lives, they need to understand how these scientific explanations are constructed, justified, and debated. Because of this relevance to everyday life, becoming scientifically literate is important for all learners, not just those who continue on to have careers in the sciences. Furthermore, the ability to consider and critique alternative explanations ties directly to twenty-first century skills, including adaptability, communication, and problem solving. It is important for schools to foster these skills in the next generation, due to applicability across different job contexts and real-world situations.

Understand the Nature of Science

Engaging in scientific explanations can also help shift students' views of science from a static set of facts to a body of knowledge that has been socially created by scientists and constantly changes and grows with new innovations and discoveries. Viewing science as just a set of facts to memorize can discourage some students from being interested in science and pursuing it further in school as a career. Instead, science is actually filled with dispute as scientists debate and try to better understand the world around us. For example, scientists investigate how eating and other health choices influence human aging and disease. One decade-long study of rhesus monkeys investigates how a reduced calorie diet impacts age-related disorders such as cancer, diabetes, and heart disease and brain atrophy in monkeys. Although there are positive effects for monkeys, scientists debate the potential implications in terms of humans. Furthermore, questions remain whether it is just calorie restriction or if it is the removal of certain types of foods that would be most important in reducing the probability of certain diseases in humans. The field of public health is full of debate as scientists try to better understand the human body and how our choices impact our health. Introducing students to some of these debates in science as well as engaging students in debates where they have to justify their claims with evidence can help students see how knowledge is constructed in science and that science is a dynamic and creative field.

Other Classroom Benefits

Besides improving students' understandings and abilities, integrating this type of writing and conversation into your science class also provides other benefits. When students justify their claims with evidence and reasoning, you gain insight into students' thinking and understanding. You can see and hear how students understand the science concepts and how students apply those science concepts to make sense of the world around them. These insights serve as an essential formative assessment tool that you can use to adapt your own instruction and more closely meet the needs of your students. Scientific explanation tasks also serve as important summative tools, in both classrooms and on state standardized tests, to evaluate whether students have developed flexible and usable science knowledge. This type of science writing, which requires students to justify their claims, is frequently included in the open-ended items on state standardized tests. For example, Brandon's revised scientific explanation for fat and soap would be much more likely to receive a higher score on a state standardized test than his first explanation, because of his use of scientific evidence and reasoning.

Integrating scientific explanations into the science curriculum also provides an excellent literacy connection and opportunity for writing across the content areas (Moje, Peek-Brown, Sutherland, Marx, Blumenfeld, & Krajcik, 2004; Sutherland, McNeill, Krajcik, & Colson, 2006). This type of persuasive writing is an important genre of academic writing that often receives less attention in K-12 schools in the United States; instead, schools often focus on personal narrative or storytelling (Purcell-Gates, Duke, & Martineau, 2007). Incorporating scientific explanations into your classroom instruction provides an excellent opportunity for analytic writing that includes the use of evidence. Connecting writing scientific explanations to students' other classes, such as English and Social Studies, can help students integrate and apply what they are learning in all their classes. Other classes also frequently use evidence to support claims; it is just that "what counts" as evidence in English class (e.g., a quote form a novel) is different from "what counts" as evidence in science. In fact, the common core standards for English Language Arts for grades 6-12 developed by the Council of Chief State School Officers and the National Governors Association (2010) lists argumentation in which students use evidence and reasons to support claims as a common core standard for writing. Students need support and practice in evidence-based persuasive writing across the different content areas.

Because of the key role of scientific explanations in science, they are prevalent in the national standards as well as many state standards. The national standards documents, *Benchmarks for Science Literacy* (American Association for the Advancement of Science, 1993; 2009) and *National Science Education Standards* (National Research Council, 1996), advocate the importance of scientific explanation, evidence, and argument in science classrooms. For example, the *Benchmarks for Science Literacy* state, "Present a brief scientific explanation orally or in writing that includes a claim and the evidence and reasoning that supports the claim." (12D/M6**) and the *National Science Education Standards* state, "Communicate scientific procedures and explanations" (A: 1/7, 5–8). These standards stress the importance of having students create explanations in writing and talk in science classrooms. The *Benchmarks* further elaborate some of the components that should be included in an explanation such as the evidence and reasoning to support the claim. Both documents also discuss the importance of students' critical analysis of multiple explanations. For example, the *Benchmarks* state, "Notice and criticize the reasoning in arguments in which the claims are not consistent with the evidence given" (12E/M5b*) and the *National Science Education Standards* state, "Recognize and analyze alternative explanations and predictions" (A: 1/6, 5–8). Both of these national standards stress the importance of considering and critiquing multiple explanations for the same phenomena. Appendix 1A includes a complete list of the standards from *Benchmarks for Science Literacy* and Appendix 1B from the *National Science Education Standards* that align with the goals we have been discussing around scientific explanation.

In a follow-up document to the *National Science Education Standards*, the National Research Council published *Inquiry and the National Science Education Standards* (2000) that further elaborates and clarifies the model of inquiry that they view as essential for K-12 science instruction. This document also stresses the importance of scientific explanation in science fields. The document describes five essential features of classroom inquiry:

(1) engaging in scientifically-oriented questions

(2) giving priority to evidence

(3) formulating explanations from evidence

(4) connecting explanations to scientific knowledge, and

(5) communicating and justifying explanations.

Four of the five essential features include a focus on scientific explanations.

As these examples illustrate, the importance of developing, using, and critiquing scientific explanations, evidence, and argument are prevalent throughout the standards yet the language is not always consistent. If you look at Appendix A, the AAAS *Benchmarks* discuss the importance of using claims, evidence, and reasoning in both scientific *explanations* and *arguments*. In working with teachers, we have debated whether the word *explanation* or *argument* is more accessible for elementary and middle school students as a label for this important practice. In the examples you will see throughout the book, the majority of the time the teachers chose to refer to it as scientific explanation, though there are a couple of exceptions in which the teacher or set of teachers decided to call this scientific inquiry practice scientific argument or refer to the acronym for the framework we will discuss (i.e., CER). Although we think it is important to engage students in this practice where they justify their claims with evidence and reasoning, we think it is less important whether that practice is called explanation, argument, or CER. We will refer to it as scientific explanation throughout the book to be consistent, but believe it is up to each individual teacher in terms of what they want to call this scientific inquiry practice with their students.

Student Challenges with Scientific Explanations

Although an important goal for classroom science, constructing scientific explanations presents challenges for students. Students often provide claims, but little or no justifications for those claims. These challenges can be important to keep in mind as you support your students in this complex scientific inquiry practice. Our work with teachers and classroom research (McNeill & Krajcik, 2007; McNeill et al., 2006) shows that students typically have difficulty in three different areas: (1) using appropriate and sufficient evidence, (2) providing reasoning for why their evidence supports their claim, and (3) considering alternative explanations and providing rebuttals. We have developed numerous strategies with teachers over the years to help students overcome these challenges. In future chapters, we will discuss these strategies, but first we want to summarize some of the typical student difficulties in science around justifying their claims.

Using Appropriate and Sufficient Evidence

In terms of using evidence, students often rely on their own opinions or personal experiences instead of using the data they have collected or the data that has been provided to them. For example, a group of sixth-grade students collects and analyzes data to determine whether or not the mass of an object influences how fast it falls to the earth. The students drop three different blocks that have the same volume, but different masses (e.g., 20 g., 44 g., and 142 g.) and time how long it takes the blocks to fall. The students' average data for the three blocks is 1.5 seconds, 1.7 seconds, and 1.6 seconds suggesting that mass does not affect how fast objects fall. However, the students write in their scientific explanation that heavier objects fall faster because the lightest block was a little slower and a piece of paper will take longer to hit the ground than a rock. It is important to connect students' everyday experiences, knowledge and ways of knowing to the work they conduct in science class. Yet it is also important for students to understand what counts as appropriate evidence to support a claim and that personal experiences or opinions are not always the most appropriate way to justify a claim in science. Students need to consider questions such as: What claim can I make considering the evidence I have collected? What other types of evidence do I need to support my claim?

Students also struggle at times using or considering enough data to support their claim. Sometimes students focus on one specific data point and do not consider the entire set of data and the conclusions that may be drawn from that data. For example, a group of eighth grade students investigate what area of their school has the most bacteria. They use agar plates to test multiple locations in their science classroom, the hallway, the bathroom and the cafeteria. Although on average, the agar plates from the cafeteria resulted in the most bacteria growth, the students conclude that the bathroom has the most bacteria. Most of the agar plates from the bathroom had little growth, but one plate from the handle of the sink resulted in high bacteria growth. The students focus on the results from this one plate to form their conclusion. Students need help thinking about and making sense of all of the data they have collected. Furthermore, knowing when they have enough data to support their claims is an important ability for students to develop. Your students should consider the question: Do I have enough data to support this claim?

Providing Reasoning

When students do provide evidence to support their claims, they often struggle to articulate their reasoning for why the evidence supports the claim. Yet, providing reasoning is one of the most important capabilities we should help our students develop. Students should be using their understanding of the science concepts to select certain data to answer the question or problem. For example, when a group of seventh graders conduct an investigation focused on how many different habitats are in their schoolyard, they need to use their scientific understanding that a habitat is an area where an organism lives and grows that is able to meet the needs of the organism (e.g., food, water, and shelter). Students' understanding of habitat influences what data they collect and use to support their claim. Yet in writing their scientific explanation students often omit why they chose certain data or explain what a habitat is. For example, one seventh grade student wrote that there were three habitats in his school year and listed the organisms and the food available to the organisms in the three locations, but he did not provide his reasoning for why the presence of organisms and food are evidence of different habitats. Over years of working with and observing students, we have found that the reasoning is the most difficult component of the scientific explanation process for students (McNeill et al., 2006). They have difficulty articulating what scientific theory they used to answer the question or to select evidence to determine the answer. Students should consider questions such as: Why does the evidence support the claim? What science concept links my evidence to my claim?

Considering Alternative Explanations

Another aspect of scientific explanations that proves difficult for students is considering alternative explanations and rebuttals for why another explanation might not be appropriate. Students focus on one answer and have difficulty seeing that there are potentially multiple different ways to explain a phenomenon. No matter the complexity or simplicity of the science topic, students struggle to consider multiple explanations when investigating a particular phenomenon. This difficulty can occur when students are investigating topics as complex as genetically modified food to simpler concepts such as what causes objects to float. For example, a group of fifth grade students investigate what causes objects to float. They conduct an investigation where they drop different objects in a bucket of water and observe whether they float. The students find that all the objects that had holes in them (e.g., washer and a button) sank, so they conclude that having a hole in an object makes it sink. In actuality, the density of the object determines whether it sinks, but the students did not come up with this alternative explanation. If the students had considered this alternative explanation, this might have led them to test some additional objects. Students should have considered questions such as: What might be an alternative explanation? What other evidence would I need to test the alternative explanation? For example, since the metal washer sank, an alternative explanation could be that objects made of certain substances (e.g., metal and plastic) sink. They could test a solid piece of metal and a solid piece of plastic to determine if they sink as well.

For more complex science topics or for students with more experience, you may want them to construct a rebuttal as well, which can be challenging for students. For example, students could be investigating whether genetically modified foods are beneficial or harmful for human health. In addition to providing a justification for their position, students can be asked to construct a rebuttal that provides counter evidence and reasoning for why the alternative claim is not appropriate. For example, when a group of eighth grade students was preparing for a debate about genetically modified foods, their initial rebuttal was just that the other group was "wrong" and did not know what they were talking about. Their teacher pushed the group to consider what evidence weakened the plausibility of the alternative claim. Students should consider questions such as: Is there evidence or reasoning that suggests the alternative explanation is not appropriate or as strong of an explanation?

Students need to be able to identify and evaluate multiple potential explanations and rule out other options—a practice that is central to making decisions in various life scenarios. Supporting students in rebutting alternative explanations ultimately fosters in them an increased ability to think through various options in other life situations. This aspect of scientific explanation promotes another important aspect of twenty-first century skills—workers of the future will need to consider which is the best possible option among many choices when problem solving and when adapting to new and uncertain situations.

Check Point

Constructing scientific explanations is an essential component of science as scientists try to understand how and why different phenomena occur. Recent science education reform documents and national standards advocate for the importance of supporting students in constructing scientific explanations where they justify the claims they make with appropriate evidence and reasoning as well as consider and refute alternative explanations. Engaging students in scientific explanations can have many benefits such as helping students: (1) understand science concepts, (2) develop twenty-first century skills, (3) use evidence to support claims, (4) reason logically, (5) consider and critique alternative explanations, and (6) understand the nature of science. Yet students can have many challenges with constructing scientific explanations such as using evidence, providing reasoning, and considering alternative explanations and rebuttals. Constructing a strong scientific explanation is a challenging task and students may not have a lot of experience. Consequently, for students to succeed in this task they need multiple opportunities for practice as well as instructional support from their teachers to help them improve over time. In future chapters, we will describe how to design learning and assessment tasks as well as how to incorporate different teaching strategies into your instruction in order to help your students achieve greater success with this important scientific inquiry practice.

Study Group Questions

1. Do you think your students would benefit from constructing scientific explanations? Why or why not?
2. Examine the national standards in Appendix A and B. How do your state or district standards align with students constructing scientific explanations?
3. Think about times in the past when you have engaged your students in scientific explanations in either writing or science talk. What are some challenges that your students had with this type of writing or talk? What did you find challenging about incorporating scientific explanations into your classroom?

Appendix 1A: AAAS *Benchmarks* (2009) for Scientific Explanation

17

Appendix
1B: NRC
Standards
(1996) for
Scientific
Explanation

Scientific investigations usually involve the collection of relevant evidence, the use of logical reasoning, and the application of imagination in devising hypotheses and explanations to make sense of the collected evidence. (AAAS, 1B/M1b*)

Often different explanations can be given for the same observations, and it is not always possible to tell which one is correct. (AAAS, 12A/M3*)

Present a brief scientific explanation orally or in writing that includes a claim and the evidence and reasoning that supports the claim. 12D/M6**

Seek to gain a better understanding of a scientific idea by asking for an explanation, restating an explanation in a different way, and asking questions when some aspect of an explanation is not clear. 12D/M7**

Explain a scientific idea to someone else, checking understanding and responding to questions. 12D/M8**

Question claims based on vague attributions (such as "Leading doctors say . . . ") or on statements made by celebrities or others outside the area of their particular expertise. 12E/M1

Be skeptical of claims based on very small samples or biased samples. 12E/M3*

Notice and criticize the reasoning in arguments in which fact and opinion are intermingled. 12E/M5a

Notice and criticize the reasoning in arguments in which the claims are not consistent with the evidence given. 12E/M5b*

Be skeptical of claims based only on analogies. 12E/M5c*

Notice and criticize the reasoning in arguments in which no mention is made of whether control groups are used or whether the control groups are very much like the experimental group. 12E/M5d*

Be skeptical of arguments in which all members of a group (such as teenagers or chemists) are implied to have nearly identical characteristics that differ from those of other groups. 12E/M5e

Source: Reprinted with permission from the American Association for the Advancement of Science Project 2061. www.project2061.org/publications/bsl/online/index.php.

Appendix 1B: NRC *Standards* (1996) for Scientific Explanation

Develop . . . explanations . . . using evidence. (NRC, 1996, A: 1/4, 5–8)

Think critically and logically to make the relationships between evidence and explanation. (NRC, 1996, A: 1/5, 5–8)

Recognize and analyze alternative explanations and predictions. (NRC, 1996, A: 1/6, 5–8)

Communicate scientific procedures and explanations. (NRC, 1996, A: 1/7, 5–8)

Scientific explanations emphasize evidence, have logically consistent arguments, and use scientific principles, models and theories. The scientific community accepts and uses such explanations until displaced by better scientific ones. When such displacement occurs, science advances. (NRC, A2/5:5–8)

Science advances through legitimate skepticism. Asking questions and querying other scientists' explanations is part of scientific inquiry. Scientists evaluate the explanations proposed by other scientists by examining evidence, comparing evidence, identify faulty reasoning pointing out statements that go beyond the evidence, and suggesting alternative explanations for the same observations. (NRC, A2/6:5–8)

Source: Reprinted with permission from National Science Education Standards, 1996 by the National Academy of Sciences, Courtesy of the National Academies Press, Washington, D.C.

Framework for Constructing Scientific Explanations

What does it mean to construct a scientific explanation? What are the important features of scientific writing? How can you introduce those features to your students? Let's consider the following vignette from Mr. Lyon's eighth-grade classroom.

Mr. Lyon's eighth-grade physical science class is examining what it means when a chemical reaction occurs, or more specifically, is discovering that a chemical reaction produces a new substance with different properties. Groups in his class dissolve a white powder in water to form a clear and transparent solution, then dissolve another white powder in water to form another clear and transparent solution. Student groups then pour the two clear liquids together and see a thick yellow solid that collects at the bottom of the test tube. Mr. Lyon hears several students say, "Cool," and "Where did that stuff come from?" Mr. Lyon then asks the groups to work together to write a scientific explanation that answers the question: Did a new substance form when the two solutions were poured together? He writes on the board:

A scientific explanation has three parts:
  • *Claim: a conclusion to a question or problem*
  • *Evidence: scientific data that supports the claim*
  • *Reasoning: a justification that links the evidence to the claim (use scientific principles to make that claim)*

He then tells the class to write their explanation and to place their explanation on an overhead transparency. After the students finish discussing and writing their explanation, Mr. Lyon asks one of the groups to share their scientific explanation for class critique. Tonya, Shawn, and Miki volunteer to share their explanation. They place their explanation on the overhead and read it out loud:

> *We think a new substance formed because a solid yellow material formed when we poured the two solutions together.*

Mr. Lyon asks Tonya, Shawn, and Miki, "What is the claim in your explanation?" Miki answers, "Our claim is that a new substance formed." Mr. Lyon circles this part of their explanation and asks the class if they agree with this claim. All the student groups answer in unison: "Yeah."

> *We think a new substance formed because a solid yellow formed when we poured the two solutions together.*

Mr. Lyon then asks Tonya, Shawn, and Miki, "What is your evidence?" Shawn responds by saying, "A yellow solid formed."
Mr. Lyon underlines this part of their explanation and asks the class, "Do you agree with their evidence? Is there anything else they should add to their evidence?" Several students raise their hands.

> *We think a new substance formed because a solid yellow formed when we poured the two solutions together.*

Mr. Lyon calls on Owen. Owen says, "They also need to add that before there wasn't a solid present in the solutions. This shows a change from a solution to solid. Also, the solutions started as clear. The yellow shows a change in color." Other students agree that both pieces of information are important evidence for their claim.
Next, Mr. Lyon asks Tonya, Shawn, and Miki, "What is your reasoning in your explanation?" Tonya responds, "We forgot to include the reasoning." Miki adds, "You can tell since you circled the claim and underlined the evidence. There is nothing left to be the reasoning." Mr. Lyon then asks them

again, "What can you add as the reasoning? Why does your evidence support your claim? Remember to make sure you include scientific principles." Miki volunteers, "The solid yellow substance has difference properties." Mr. Lyon asks, "Anything else?" The group answers sheepishly, "We don't think so." Mr. Lyon then asks the class if they would add anything else. Several groups raise their hands.

This scenario illustrates how a middle school teacher can support students in writing scientific explanations. Mr. Lyon broke the complex task of writing a scientific explanation into three components (i.e., a claim, evidence, and reasoning), provided practice for students in writing explanations, and encouraged peer review.

This chapter will help you understand how you can introduce scientific explanations to your students using a framework we developed with grade 5–8 teachers to support students in constructing scientific explanations. Although many of the examples focus on students' written scientific explanations, you can also use the framework in classroom discussions or small group work when students are trying to make sense of scientific data. We describe the framework first and then provide examples of student writing and videos to illustrate how to introduce the framework to your students.

Students' Understandings of Scientific Explanations

When we ask students to construct a scientific explanation, the word *explanation* might have very different meanings to students than we might intend them to have. The students' understanding of a scientific explanation does not necessarily match our expectations in terms of what we are hoping they will include in their writing and talk. When scientists create explanations, they are trying to understand how or why different phenomena occur, such as global climate change. Furthermore, scientists use evidence to support and justify their claims. Students' intuitive understandings of scientific explanations often do not include either of these ideas. Rather, students may view explanations as just describing and summarizing. For example, in interviews with fifth-grade students, we asked them: "What do you think it means for a scientist to create an explanation?" The students' responses often focused on an exchange between people, such as "if they tell somebody, like all the people, like in public that they learned something like new." In other instances, students spoke about describing or observations, such as "they try to explain um what they're doing, sort of like observing, describing what they see and what they're doing."

When asked about creating an explanation in science class, many students also talked about an exchange between people or observations. Unfortunately, almost half the students interviewed simply said that they did not know what it means to create a scientific explanation in school. Students' responses suggest that when we ask them for a scientific explanation in class, they tend to be unclear of what exactly to include in their writing, so we need to guide them in the process. It is important to help them understand what it means to write a scientific explanation.

Framework for Constructing Scientific Explanations

The instructional framework for scientific explanation provides students with guidelines for what to include in their science writing, oral presentations, and classroom discussions. The framework can change students' understanding of what it means to create an explanation in science and in their science classroom. By making the implicit rules of science explicit, the framework helps students see how to justify claims in science. We developed it for a certain type of science writing and talking: to encourage students to answer a question or problem using data given to them or that they collected themselves.

To develop the framework, we adapted Stephen Toulmin's (1958) model of argumentation that has been used by other science educators to support students in both writing (Bell & Linn, 2000; Berland & Reiser, 2009) and talk (Erduran, Simon, & Osborne, 2004; Jiménez-Aleixandre, Rodríguez, & Duschl, 2000). Toulmin's argumentation model is also used in other content areas, such as social studies and language arts, and is frequently used in composition courses. Although we use Toulmin's basic structure, we adapt the language to be more accessible for students. Our scientific explanation framework consists of four components: (1) claim, (2) evidence, (3) reasoning,[1] and (4) rebuttal.

Depending on the experience, understanding, and age of your students, you may want to start by introducing your students to the first three components of claim, evidence, and reasoning. When your students have more experience, you may then add the final component of the rebuttal, which is the most complex part of constructing a scientific explanation. Figure 2.1 displays the relationship between the claim, evidence, and reasoning. This figure illustrates how the evidence supports the claim and the reasoning provides a justification for that link between the claim and evidence. We begin by discussing the claim, evidence, and reasoning as well as the relationship between these three components.

We then add on the fourth component, the rebuttal. We discuss the role of the rebuttal in scientific explanation in terms of how it considers and rules out alternative explanations for a scientific phenomenon.

---

[1]The reasoning combines Toulmin's warrant and backing.

FIGURE 2.1

Claim, Evidence, and Reasoning

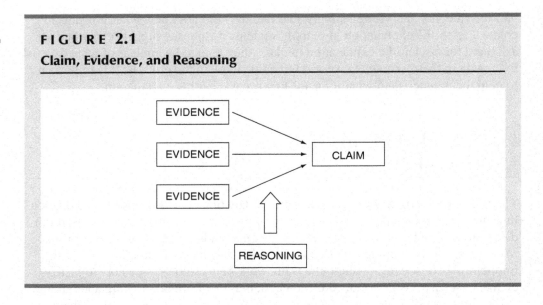

Claim

The claim is a statement that expresses the answer or conclusion to a question
or problem. Typically, we have found that this is the easiest part for students to
include in their writing, though younger students can still find this aspect challenging. When provided with a question about data students have just collected or
data that has been given to them, we ask them to construct a claim that addresses
the question. For example, in Chapter 1 we discussed Brandon's two explanations
about whether soap and fat are the same or different substances. In both Brandon's
initial explanation and his revised explanation, he included an accurate claim that
fat and soap are different substances. Table 2.1 shows the breakdown of Brandon's
revised explanation in terms of claim, evidence, and reasoning. For some students
in Brandon's class, the claim was actually all they wrote in their initial explanation.
They simply stated a claim without any justification. Other times, particularly with
younger students, students may write a claim, but it does not specifically answer the
question posed. For example, in answer to the question posed to Brandon's class a
student could write, "Fat and soap have different densities." Although this statement
is true, it does not answer the original question of whether fat and soap are the same
substance. Consequently, it is important to encourage students to look specifically
at what the question is asking. The claim provides the conclusion or answer to that
question. The other components of the scientific explanation framework provide
the justification for that claim. Figure 2.1 illustrates how the other two components
(evidence and reasoning) support the claim.

*majority of
7th grade
at SBP*

Component	Brandon's Revised Explanation
TABLE 2.1 Brandon's Revised Explanation as Claim, Evidence, and Reasoning	
Claim	Fat and soap are different substances.
Evidence	Fat is off-white and soap is milky white. (#1) Fat is soft-squishy and soap is hard. (#2) Fat is soluble in oil, but soap is not soluble. Soap is soluble in water, but fat is not. (#3) Fat has a melting point of 47°C and soap has a melting point above 100°C. (#4) Fat has a density of 0.92 g/cm³ and soap has a density of 0.84 g/cm³. (#5)
Reasoning	These are all properties. Because fat and soap have different properties, I know they are different.

Evidence

Evidence is scientific data that supports the claim. Data are information such as observations and measurements that come from natural settings (e.g., behavior of birds) and results from controlled experiments (e.g., speed of objects falling). One of the key characteristics of science is its use of scientific data as evidence to understand the natural world (National Research Council, 2000). The accuracy or reliability of scientific data are often checked through multiple trials or by comparing different types of data. Students can either collect data themselves or be provided with data such as data tables, readings, or a database. When students are provided with data, this is sometimes referred to as secondhand data because the students did not collect the data themselves, rather, the data were collected by experts (Hug & McNeill, 2008). Secondhand data are often used when it is not possible for students to collect data themselves, such as when the phenomenon is too small (e.g., atoms and molecules), too large (e.g., the solar system), or takes too long of a period of time (e.g., evolution). Once students have reliable data, they need to make sense of that data. Students should use their data as evidence to come up with and support their claim to the original question or problem. Figure 2.1 illustrates how multiple pieces of evidence provide support for a claim.

When initially introducing the idea of evidence in a scientific explanation to your students, you may want to focus on the importance of using data, such as observations and measurements, to make and support claims. Instead of relying on evidence to support their claims, students often use their opinions, beliefs, and everyday experiences, even if they spent considerable time collecting and organizing their data. Students require support to understand the important role of evidence in answering questions in science. Any conclusion or claim they make about the natural world should be linked to specific and systematic evidence. As your students become more comfortable using evidence to support their claims, discussions about the characteristics of evidence may be deepened *discuss/talking about reliability of data*

to include considerations about whether the data are *appropriate* and *sufficient* to justify the claim.

Appropriate data need to be scientifically relevant for supporting the claim. For example, in the soap and fat example in Brandon's initial explanation he included the fact that soap and fat are used for different things (washing and cooking) as evidence that they are different substances. This is not appropriate evidence for his claim because sometimes a single substance (e.g., aluminum) can be used for creating two objects with different functions (e.g., a soda can and a car). Consequently, what a substance is used for is not appropriate evidence for his claim. In his revised explanation, he uses color, hardness, solubility, melting point, and density as evidence. These are all appropriate pieces of evidence for his claim because all five characteristics are properties; properties are characteristics that are independent of the amount of the sample and can be used to identify substances. For example, the melting point of a substance (such as ice) will be the same whether one has a large amount or a small amount of the substance. Properties are scientifically relevant data for supporting the claim that the substances are the same or different and as such they are appropriate. Often in science we have a lot of data and need to determine which data we should and should not use to answer a particular question or problem. Determining what is and is not appropriate evidence can be challenging for students, yet it is a critical skill that students need to develop for scientific literacy in the world in which they live.

scientific literacy

Sufficient data means a student has gathered enough data to support his or her claim. Typically in science, we collect, analyze, and use multiple pieces of data to answer a particular question or problem. Figure 2.1 illustrates three pieces of evidence supporting the claim, but in reality the number of pieces of evidence required will depend on the particular situation. For example, in Brandon's revised scientific explanation he includes five pieces of evidence to support his claim. Usually, one piece of evidence is not sufficient and students will need to figure out how many pieces of evidence to use to support their claim. This can be challenging for students, because they may want to focus on only one piece of evidence. Determining if there are sufficient and appropriate data for a claim are critical aspects of constructing scientific explanations and help build scientific literacy.

Reasoning

In terms of the first three components (claim, evidence, and reasoning), reasoning is the most difficult step in the framework because it involves providing a justification that links the evidence to the claim. This is why in Figure 2.1 we have the reasoning arrow pointing at that link between the claim and evidence. The reasoning explains why the evidence supports the claim, providing a logical connection between the evidence and claim. Typically, the reasoning requires the discussion of appropriate scientific principles to explain that link, because when you are picking or using scientific data you make your decisions based on your understanding of the scientific principles. The reasoning should articulate the logic behind that choice.

For example, in Brandon's explanation, he used color, hardness, solubility, melting point, and density as evidence that fat and soap are different substances. Someone could question him on why he chose that particular evidence. They might ask: Why didn't you use volume? Why didn't you use mass? Brandon's reasoning should explain why he chose that particular evidence. His revised explanation does provide some reasoning for his choice in that he wrote, "These are all properties. Because fat and soap have different properties, I know they are different." This provides some reasoning for his choice, but he could actually have described it in more detail. This is the logic behind his choice: *Color, melting point, solubility, and density are properties. Properties are characteristics of a substance that do not change even if the amount of the substance changes and can be used to determine if two things are the same substance. Since the properties are different, I know they are different substances.*

Students struggle with using scientific principles and describing their logic behind why their evidence supports their claim. Helping students learn how to articulate their reasoning can help them better understand their own thinking as well as develop a stronger understanding of the science content. Although it can be challenging for students, helping them develop sound reasoning skills is critical for their development of scientific literacy. It will not only help them develop better explanations, it will also help them analyze the flaws of other arguments such as those found in the newspaper or on the web.

Rebuttal

The last component of the scientific explanation framework is the rebuttal. Figure 2.2 illustrates how the rebuttal connects to the other three components of claim, evidence, and reasoning. The rebuttal recognizes and describes alternative explanations and provides counter evidence and reasoning for why the alternative is not the appropriate explanation for the question or problem. Often in science there are multiple plausible explanations for how or why something has occurred. Scientists consider and debate these multiple possibilities. In critiquing alternative explanations, they go through a similar process as when they are creating an explanation. Scientists consider the alternative claim as well as the evidence and reasoning for that claim. In constructing their final scientific explanation, they will explain not only why they believe claim 1 is correct, but also why they believe alternative claim 2 is incorrect. For instance, they might argue that the evidence that is provided is inappropriate for supporting the claim. The rebuttal includes the explanation for why they believe claim 2 is not correct.

Most teachers introducing the scientific explanation framework do not initially include the concept of a rebuttal. For example, when Brandon's teacher initially introduced the framework for scientific explanation, he only discussed claim, evidence, and reasoning. When Brandon revised his explanation, he was asked to include those three components, but not a rebuttal. This idea that there can be multiple alternative explanations for the same question in science can be challenging for students as well as for teachers who do not have experience

FIGURE 2.2

Claim, Evidence, Reasoning, and Rebuttal

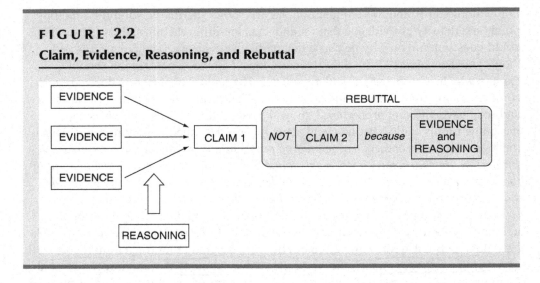

with taking into consideration alternative explanations. Consequently, depending on the experiences of your students you may want to begin with just claim, evidence, and reasoning and then add on the concept of rebuttal after students have become more comfortable with the first three components.

Supporting students in making claims, using evidence and reasoning, and taking into consideration alternative explanations when writing scientific explanations is difficult for students to learn and challenging for teachers to help students understand. However, helping students learn this important practice will give them an invaluable tool to use throughout their lives.

Video Example—Introducing the Instructional Framework

We now use a video example to illustrate how you can introduce the framework to your students and what type of language makes sense for grade 5–8 students. The video for Chapter 2 on the DVD is from a seventh-grade science classroom where the teacher, Ms. Nelson, was introducing the framework for scientific explanation to her students. As the vignette in Chapter 1 illustrated, Ms. Nelson's students had been collecting water quality data from a local stream and are investigating the question: What is the water quality of our stream? In writing up the results from their investigation, Ms. Nelson planned for her students to make a claim about the quality of the stream and then write a justification for that claim using the data they had collected and what they had learned about water quality. Consequently, before she had them complete the write-up she devoted one lesson to introducing and discussing the framework for scientific explanation.

Ms. Nelson chose to introduce the first three components—claim, evidence, and reasoning—of the framework. Watch the 10-minute video clip from this lesson (video clip 2.1). Ms. Nelson uses a variety of strategies during the introduction of the framework to help students develop an understanding of claim, evidence, and reasoning and to link this framework to their prior experiences.

Introducing Claim

The clip begins with Ms. Nelson writing the word "Claim" on the board and she then asks her students, "Anyone have any idea what a claim is? What is a claim? In your everyday life." She has a number of students share their ideas before she combines a couple of them in the following definition of what claim is: "Statement that answers a question." Throughout this introduction of the scientific explanation framework, Ms. Nelson uses this technique of eliciting student ideas before providing them with the definition of each of the three components. She has in a binder (that you can see her look at a couple of times during the video clip) definitions that she wants the students to come up with as a class. Instead, she could very simply have written the three definitions on the board and the introduction would have been quicker. Rather, her strategy encourages student reflection and ownership of the framework and her technique encourages students to think about the words and connect them to their prior experiences. Ms. Nelson's strategy is student-centered. But although she encourages students to share their ideas, the focus is not to support student-to-student discussion of the ideas; student-to-student interaction is a strategy she uses at other times, which we will illustrate in Chapter 7.

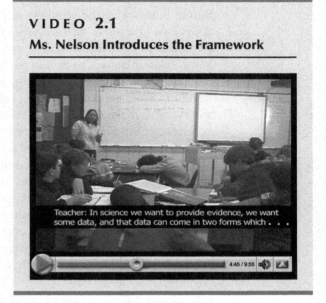

VIDEO 2.1

Ms. Nelson Introduces the Framework

Teacher: In science we want to provide evidence, we want some data, and that data can come in two forms which . . .

4:45 / 9:55

The Claim Answers a Question

After coming up with the definition of a claim, Ms. Nelson then focuses on the importance of the claim answering a question. Making sure the claim specifically answers the question instead of a different, but related, question can be very challenging for students. This conversation encourages Ms. Nelson's students to think about this important characteristic of the claim. Furthermore, she uses everyday examples to help students think about how the framework relates to their lives. She provides example claims such as "Brett Favre is the best quarterback that ever lived" and "We had a great field hockey game yesterday." Throughout the discussion of the other two components, she returns to everyday examples to help students understand the meaning of each component, because she wants to connect the framework to what students already know in terms of how to figure out or prove the answer to a question. Throughout the rest of the school year and during the next year in eighth-grade Ms. Nelson's students will have many opportunities to apply the framework to science examples.

Introducing Evidence

The next section of the video clip shifts to discussing the evidence component. Before introducing the word *evidence*, Ms. Nelson first elicits her students' ideas about how you prove or back up a claim in your everyday life as well as in science. Her students come up with the importance of using "facts" and "data," which Ms. Nelson then uses to introduce the term *evidence*. One of the students in her class then brings up another example and asks if this idea of claims and evidence is similar to what happens in the presidential debates.[2] This illustrates that the students are trying to make sense of these different components and connect them to their life experiences. As Ms. Nelson discusses the presidential example, she provides a definition of *evidence* that she writes on the board: "data that supports that claim." You will notice as she discusses the components she writes key terms and definitions on the board so that students have a visual representation as well as the classroom talk to support them in building an understanding. Furthermore, Ms. Nelson has asked the students to record these definitions in their science notebooks. The act of writing can help students remember the components and they will have a permanent record that they can return to when they are asked to write scientific explanations for their different science investigations in the future.

Different Characteristics of Evidence

After introducing the idea of evidence, Ms. Nelson continues to discuss different characteristics of evidence. First she asks students about different categories of data. Specifically, she has students come up with the idea that data can be either quantitative or qualitative. Then she asks students how much data they would want to include. One student responds, "You need to have enough so that you can prove it." Ms. Nelson builds on this idea to discuss the fact that you want to use multiple pieces of data as evidence to support the claim. Ms. Nelson's students are seventh-grade students who have had some experiences in the past using evidence in science. Consequently, this level of complexity works well with her students. As we will discuss later in this chapter (Table 2.3) there are a variety of different levels of

---

[2]This video clip was recorded in October 2008 during the John McCain and Barack Obama presidential debates.

complexity in terms of the framework that you may want to use with your students, depending on their prior experiences.

Introducing Reasoning

Finally, Ms. Nelson introduces the concept of reasoning. In discussing this component, she introduces a new everyday claim: "I could be an NFL quarterback." She uses this example because it is a claim that her students think is not accurate. As soon as she says it, some of the students smile and a couple of the students laugh. She provides evidence for this claim, but then goes on to talk about how the reasoning is faulty. She provides the following evidence: when she was younger she played football every Saturday, she was the quarterback, she had a 65 percent completion rate and has been watching football her entire life. Although this is all evidence around football and it shows that she was a quarterback, the evidence does not prove that she could be an NFL quarterback. This illustrates the importance of the reasoning for appropriately justifying a claim. She also provides a science example from a previous experience they had in class. Furthermore, Ms. Nelson defines the reasoning in terms of science: "Use the science ideas or concepts to show how the evidence supports the claim." Similar to the other two components of the framework, she has the students discuss and share their ideas before providing them with a concrete definition.

The claim, evidence, and reasoning framework is a lot for a grade 5–8 student to process in one 10-minute introduction or during one science class. But Ms. Nelson's goal is not that her students will have a complete and thorough understanding by the end of the period. Rather, it is an introduction to a complex framework they will revisit and build on throughout this school year and in future years. Students now have a new tool that they will be using over and over again across the year as they engage in science writing and discussion. She provides her students with a common framework and language that they can now use whenever they are trying to answer questions in their science classroom and in their everyday lives.

Examples of Scientific Explanations

To further illustrate the scientific explanation framework, we discuss examples from across the different science content areas—physics, chemistry, biology, and earth science. Table 2.2 provides each example broken down into the four components—claim, evidence, reasoning, and rebuttal. Table 2.2 also includes the question that the scientific explanation addresses. Each example increases in complexity from the physics example through the earth science example to illustrate the flexibility of the framework and how it can be used in different contexts. The most complex example we provide is in earth science; however, that is not to say that all earth science scientific explanations are going to be more complex than physics explanations.

TABLE 2.2 Examples of the Different Components for Scientific Explanations

Question	Claim	Evidence	Reasoning	Rebuttal
Physics Does mass affect how quickly an object falls?	No, mass does not affect how quickly an object falls.	The blocks had different masses—20 g, 30 g., 44 g, 123 g, and 142 g. But the average time for all five blocks was about the same—between 1.5 and 1.8 seconds.	Since the blocks had different masses but took about the same time to fall, I know that mass does not affect how quickly something falls.	Some people may think mass is important, because a piece of paper would fall slower than a baseball. But there must be another characteristic of the paper besides mass, which is why it falls more slowly.
Chemistry What type of process took place (mixing, phase change, or chemical reaction)?	A chemical reaction occurred.	Before, the penny was brownish in color, was not soluble in water, and had a density of 8.96 g/cm^3. After the experiment, the green solid was formed, soluble in water, and had a density of 1.88 g/cm^3. The color, solubility, and density changed.	Color, solubility, and density are all properties. Since the properties changed, I know a new substance was made, which means a chemical reaction occurred. Chemical reactions create new substances that have different properties from the old substances.	Another explanation could be that a mixture was created or a third explanation could be that a phase change occurred. Since there is a new substance, it cannot be a mixture or a phase change. A mixture would just be a combination of the old substances and a phase change would be the same substance in a different state.
Biology What will happen to the shark population if the phytoplankton population dies out?	The shark population will die out.	The shark eats other fish such as the ocean fish and the lantern fish. The ocean fish and the lantern fish eat other organisms such as shrimp and copepods. The shrimp and copepods eat the phytoplankton.	Phytoplankton are producers and they make their own food using energy from the sun. All the other organisms in the food web depend on the phytoplankton, even if they do not directly eat them. If the phytoplankton die, primary consumers (shrimp and copepods) will die because they will have no food, which will cause the secondary consumers (ocean fish and lantern fish) to die, which will cause the shark to die.	You might think the shark population would not change, because they do not eat the phytoplankton. But they will actually die out because they eat organisms that eat the phytoplankton.
Earth Science How was the Grand Canyon formed?	The Grand Canyon was mainly formed by water cutting into and eroding the soil.	The soil in the Grand Canyon is hard, cannot absorb water, and has few plants to hold it in place. When it rains in the Grand Canyon it can rain very hard and cause flash floods. The flash floods come down the side of the Grand Canyon and into the Colorado River.	Water moving can cause erosion. Erosion is the movement of materials on the earth's surface. In terms of the Grand Canyon, the water moved the soil and rock from the sides of the Grand Canyon into the Colorado River where it was then washed away.	Some people may think the Grand Canyon was caused by a large earthquake, but the Grand Canyon is not near any tectonic plate boundaries. Furthermore, earthquakes in Colorado are rare and do not tend to be very large—largest earthquake on record had a magnitude of 6.6.

We could have used any of the four different content areas to illustrate either the simplest or most complex example. We wanted to illustrate the range so you could consider what level of complexity might be appropriate to introduce this framework to your students. In the next chapter, we discuss how to design these and other learning tasks to provide students with the opportunity to construct scientific explanations.

Physics Example

Physics provides many opportunities for students to collect data, analyze data, and write scientific explanations in which they make sense of the data and justify their claims. A variety of topics in physics lend themselves to students conducting first-hand investigations where they either collect data or are provided with data to make sense of such as force, friction, gravity, air resistance, motion, electricity, magnetism, light, and energy. The physics example in Table 2.2 comes from an investigation to answer the question: Does mass affect how quickly an object falls? In this investigation, students drop five blocks that are all the same size and shape but have different masses.[3] This example in Table 2.2 illustrates a simpler scientific explanation for a couple of different reasons. First, there are only two possible claims—either that mass does or does not affect how quickly objects fall. In this case, the correct claim is that mass does not affect how quickly an object falls. The students then have two different types of evidence to support their claim: (1) the mass of the different objects and (2) how quickly the objects fall. The reasoning then links the claim and evidence without having to draw from students' understanding of the scientific principles outside of this specific investigation. They can answer this question by analyzing the data they have just collected. For example, a student's reasoning might state: *Since the blocks have different masses but took about the same time to fall, I know that mass does not affect how quickly something falls*. Finally, the rebuttal brings up a counterclaim, but does not refute it in depth: *Some people may think mass is important, because a piece of paper would fall slower than a baseball. But there must be another characteristic of the paper besides mass, which is why it falls more slowly*. In order to provide a strong rebuttal, the student would need to do further investigations exploring other characteristics of the objects. This is an example where you could choose not to have students include a rebuttal, but rather focus on the claim, evidence, and reasoning.

The main reason we classified this as a simple scientific explanation is because the question is very focused. If you want to have students write a more complex scientific explanation around the same science concepts, you could use a more open question such as: What characteristics of an object affect how fast it falls? or Why does a piece of paper fall slower than a baseball? Both of these questions could result in multiple possible claims (not just two), a range of evidence looking at

---

[3]The blocks have different masses because they are made of different substances. For example, students could have five blocks made of wood, plastic, aluminum, iron, and copper.

different characteristics of objects, reasoning that includes science concepts such as gravity and air resistance, and a more complex rebuttal that explicitly refutes other potential explanations.

Chemistry Example

Chemistry also offers a variety of opportunities for students to write scientific explanations. In grades 5–8, students can conduct investigations or be provided with data around topics such as substances, properties, chemical reactions, phase changes, states of matter, mixtures, and conservation of matter. The example in Table 2.2 is a scientific explanation for an investigation in which students are answering the question: What type of process took place (mixing, phase change, or chemical reaction)? They have placed a penny in a container with vinegar overnight. The next day there is a green solid on the penny. Students use data about the two solids (penny and green solid) to determine whether the green substance was the result of a chemical reaction, a phase change, or mixing. In the physics example, there were two basic claims that a student could construct. The wording of this question expands the possible claims to include three scientific processes. The correct claim is that a chemical reaction occurred. The evidence is the color, solubility, and density data that is different for the two substances. The reasoning in this example is more complex than the physics example. In this example, the student needs to explain what a chemical reaction is (i.e., a process that creates new substances) and why they know a chemical reaction occurred (i.e., the properties changed, which means that a new substance was created). In order to provide the link between the evidence and claim, the student needs to explain the scientific principles they used to make sense of the data. Finally, the rebuttal explains why the investigation was a chemical reaction as opposed to mixing or a phase change by providing reasoning that describes the scientific ideas around these two processes: *Since there is a new substance, it cannot be a mixture or a phase change. A mixture would just be a combination of the old substances and a phase change would be the same substance in a different state.* Similar to the physics example, you can decide whether or not to ask your students to include the rebuttal depending on their experience and expertise with scientific explanations.

Biology Example

Scientific explanations in biology can occur after students conduct controlled experiments, but they also may focus on explaining observations of living organisms. Scientific explanations in the life sciences may focus on topics such as needs of living things, life cycles, adaptations, animal behavior, population dynamics (e.g., predator/prey relationships), organ systems, diseases, and heredity. For instance, the example in Table 2.2 is based on an activity where students examined data about the eating patterns of organisms in a marine ecosystem. Students were asked to write a scientific explanation answering the following question: What will happen to the shark population if the phytoplankton population dies out? Phytoplankton are the only producers and the shark is the top consumer in the marine food web. In this example, there are numerous potential claims that students could make, such as the population of shark will stay the same, increase, decrease, or die out. The correct claim is that the shark population will also die out. The evidence in this example consists of the data about which organisms eat other organisms in the marine ecosystem. This is different evidence than the physics and chemistry examples that consisted of results from an experiment. Here the evidence is observations about the behaviors of organisms. Furthermore, those observations, such as a shark eating an ocean sunfish, are not directly observable by students so they need to rely on data collected by other individuals (i.e., secondhand data). Students use information from readings and texts to gather evidence about the behavior of the organisms. In order to make sense of this evidence, students may first want to create a food web using the information to create a representation of the data. Representations play a key role in science. In other activities, students may want to create a table or graph of their data before writing their scientific explanations. Different ways of organizing and representing data can help students make sense of that data before they formulate their scientific explanation. The reasoning in this example is complex, because it explains not only the role of the phytoplankton as producers in the food web, but also how removing the phytoplankton will influence the other links in the food web. Finally, the rebuttal discusses why the shark population would not stay the same, which could be assumed because the sharks do not eat phytoplankton.

Earth Science Example

Similar to biology, earth science examples can be based on data from controlled investigations or from observational data over time. Students could write scientific explanations around a variety of topics such as weathering, erosion, types of rocks, weather patterns, plate tectonics, movement of the planets, and phases of the moon. The earth science example in Table 2.2 answers the question: How was the Grand Canyon formed? This question is very open and allows students to provide a variety of claims. It is also a question for which students cannot directly collect data. Furthermore, the Grand Canyon has formed over the last 5 to 6 million years. Consequently, there are no human records dating back to the beginning of the Grand Canyon's formation, which makes it more difficult to use evidence to answer this question. Yet the formation of the Grand Canyon is a question that scientists have investigated and debated alternative explanations. Just like scientists, students can look at current data about the Grand Canyon to develop a potential explanation of how it was formed. For example, students can examine photos and videos to look at features of the canyon and the impact of severe weather. They can also examine data about the characteristics of the soil, topography of the land, and the path and characteristics of the Colorado River. After examining all this secondhand data, students can construct an explanation using evidence about how they think the Grand Canyon formed. In Table 2.2, the claim that is provided is that the Grand Canyon was mainly formed by water cutting into and eroding the soil. The claim is justified using evidence about the characteristics of the soil, rain, and topography of the Grand Canyon. The reasoning explains how water can cause erosion and links the characteristics of the area to water moving the soil and rock to form the Grand Canyon. Finally, one potential alternative explanation, that the Grand Canyon was formed by an earthquake, is refuted in the rebuttal. This particular example could be extended with much more detail in terms of the evidence, reasoning, and rebuttal. The actual process that formed the Grand Canyon is more complex than that described in Table 2.2. Also, your students may have many alternative ideas about how the Grand Canyon was formed. Students can research the question, collect secondhand data, and form a scientific explanation arguing for how they believe the Grand Canyon was formed. In Table 2.2, this example is the most complex of the four examples, because it occurred millions of years ago and scientists have debated multiple explanations. There are other examples in earth science that are much simpler explanations for students to construct, such as writing a scientific explanation about the identity of an unknown mineral using properties such as streak, hardness, and luster. In Table 2.2, we show you a range of examples both from different content areas and with a range of complexities to illustrate how you could have students construct a variety of different explanations based on the particular needs and experiences of your students and the science content you currently address in your curriculum.

Increasing the Complexity of the Framework Over Time

As we discussed the framework for scientific explanation, we described aspects that you can make more or less complex depending on the level and needs of your students. In Table 2.3, we present four different ways you could introduce the framework to your students. The four variations have different levels of complexity in terms of both the number of components (three or four) and the description of each component. You should consider your students' backgrounds in deciding which variation to first use to introduce the framework. After your students have written scientific explanations and had some success in this writing, you may want to then increase the complexity of the framework. You could also make a school or districtwide decision. For example, the different grade levels (grades 5–8) could each focus on a different variation of the framework in order to support students in building a more in-depth understanding over time. In order to illustrate the different variations of the framework, we provide example student scientific explanations that all relate to the overarching question: What do plants need to grow? Although all

TABLE 2.3 Variations of the Instructional Framework for Scientific Explanation

Level of Complexity	Framework Sequence	Description of Framework for Students
Simple	Variation #1 1. Claim 2. Evidence 3. Reasoning	Claim • a statement that answers the question Evidence • scientific data that supports the claim Reasoning • a justification for why the evidence supports the claim using scientific principles

	Variation #2
	1. Claim
	2. Evidence
	  • Appropriate
	  • Sufficient
	3. Reasoning
		Claim
		• a statement that answers the question
		Evidence
		• scientific data that supports the claim
		• data needs to be appropriate
		• data needs to be sufficient
		Reasoning
		• a justification for why the evidence supports the claim using scientific principles

	Variation #3
	1. Claim
	2. Evidence
	  • Appropriate
	  • Sufficient
	3. Reasoning
	  • Multiple components
		Claim
		• a statement that answers the question
		Evidence
		• scientific data that supports the claim
		• data needs to be appropriate
		• data needs to be sufficient
		Reasoning
		• a justification for why the evidence supports the claim using scientific principles
		• each piece of evidence may have a different justification for why it supports the claim

Complex	Variation #4
	1. Claim
	2. Evidence
	  • Appropriate
	  • Sufficient
	3. Reasoning
	  • Multiple components
	4. Rebuttal
		Claim
		• a statement that answers the question
		Evidence
		• scientific data that supports the claim
		• data needs to be appropriate
		• data needs to be sufficient
		Reasoning
		• a justification for why the evidence supports the claim using scientific principles
		• each piece of evidence may have a different justification for why it supports the claim
		Rebuttal
		• describes alternative explanations, and provides counter evidence and reasoning for why the alternative explanation is not appropriate.

four examples address this question, each example increases in complexity in both the structure of the scientific explanation as well as the science content used in the explanation.

Variation #1: Claim, Evidence, and Reasoning

The first variation focuses on the three components (claim, evidence, and reasoning) and provides simple definitions of each component. This variation may be appropriate for your students if you are working with younger students or if your students have had limited experiences with this type of talk and writing. When you introduce this variation, even though you mention all three components, you may want to focus your discussion on claim and evidence. If your students are not experienced with writing and talking in this format, these two components can be quite challenging for students. Once they have developed a stronger understanding of claim and evidence, you can then shift your focus to the reasoning component and emphasize that it is also important to explain why the evidence supports the claim. In terms of the plant-growth example, a potential student explanation would state:

> *The plant that received more light grew taller (CLAIM). The plant with 24 hours of light grew 20 cm. The plant with 12 hours of light only grew 8 cm (EVIDENCE). Plants require light to grow and develop. This is why the plant that received 24 hours of light grew taller (REASONING).*

This example provides a simple claim that focuses on one variable that plants need to grow—light. The student then provides evidence to support the claim from an experiment that focused solely on comparing plants that received 24 hours of light with those that received 12 hours. The actual data the students have to answer the question is not complex; rather, it is limited to support them in the sense-making process and in writing their scientific explanations. The reasoning is also fairly simple, but it encourages students to begin thinking about why their data counts as evidence to support the claim and why they would not use different evidence or construct a different claim from this data.

Variation #2: Using More Complex Evidence

Variation #2 also includes the three components, but here the definition of evidence is expanded to encourage students to think about different characteristics of the plants. Specifically, the evidence now includes the ideas of whether the evidence is appropriate and sufficient for their claim. The plant-growth example increases in complexity:

> *The plant that received more light grew more (CLAIM). On average, for the six plants that received 24 hours of light, they grew 20 cm, had six yellow flowers, had fifteen leaves, and they were all bright green. On average,*

37

Increasing
the
Complexity
of the
Framework
Over Time

*for the six plants that received 12 hours of light, they grew 8 cm, had
two yellow flowers, and had four leaves. Also, two of the plants had zero
flowers. These plants were still bright green, but they were smaller and with
fewer flowers and leaves (EVIDENCE). Plants require light to grow and
develop. This is why the plant that received 24 hours of light grew more
(REASONING).*

The claim is still limited to focus on light, but the scientific explanation example
now includes multiple pieces of evidence. Furthermore, the evidence includes both
quantitative measurements (e.g., average height, number of flowers, and number of
leaves) and qualitative observations (e.g., color of flowers and leaves). Obviously,
the data that the students collected in this case was more complicated and required
greater analysis before they could construct their initial claim.

Variation #3: Providing More Complex Reasoning

Variation #3 focuses on the three components, but we expand the reasoning
component to become more complex. The reasoning piece can become more
complex in its use of scientific principles or it can become more complex in that
different pieces of evidence require different reasoning to articulate how the evidence supports the claim. In the plant-growth example, not only does the reasoning become more complicated, but the claim that students are justifying has also
become more complex:

*Plants need water, carbon dioxide, and light to grow (CLAIM). On average,
for the six plants that received constant light, carbon dioxide, and water,
they grew 20 cm, had six yellow flowers, had fifteen leaves, and they were
all bright green. On average, for the six plants that received 12 hours of
light, limited carbon dioxide and water, they grew 8 cm, had two yellow
flowers, and had four leaves. Also, two of the plants had zero flowers. These
plants were still bright green, but they were smaller and with fewer flowers
and leaves (EVIDENCE). Photosynthesis is the process during which
green plants produce sugar from water, carbon dioxide, and light energy.
Producing sugar is essential for plant growth and development. That is why
the plants that received a constant source of water, carbon dioxide, and
light grew the most (REASONING).*

In the previous examples, the claim focused on how light affects plant
growth. This example becomes more complex in that students are being asked
to determine multiple variables that impact plant growth. This question requires
a greater understanding of the science concepts related to plant growth and
that water, carbon dioxide, and light are necessary for photosynthesis to occur.
Although we are just illustrating in these examples the writing that students

would be producing, these variations would also require an increase in complexity in terms of the question being asked and the data being collected or provided to the students.

Variation #4: Including a Rebuttal

The final variation includes a specific focus on the rebuttal. In the rebuttal students articulate why another claim would not be more appropriate to answer a question or problem and provide counter evidence and/or reasoning to support that rationale. The only difference in this example for plant growth is the last section of the explanation focused on the rebuttal:

> *Plants need water, carbon dioxide, and light to grow (CLAIM). On average, for the six plants that received constant light, carbon dioxide, and water, they grew 20 cm, had six yellow flowers, had fifteen leaves, and they were all bright green. On average, for the six plants that received 12 hours of light, limited carbon dioxide and water, they grew 8 cm, had two yellow flowers, and had four leaves. Also, two of the plants had zero flowers. These plants were still bright green, but they were smaller and with fewer flowers and leaves (EVIDENCE). Photosynthesis is the process during which green plants produce sugar from water, carbon dioxide, and light energy. Producing sugar is essential for plant growth and development. That is why the plants that received a constant source of water, carbon dioxide, and light grew the most (REASONING). Our experimental design just limited the amount of air the plants received, not specifically the amount of carbon dioxide. So you could argue that plants need water, air, and light. But we know that the process of photosynthesis requires carbon dioxide and not another gas (like oxygen), which is why we concluded specifically that the carbon dioxide was required for growth. If we could limit just the carbon dioxide in our design, we would have better evidence for this claim (REBUTTAL).*

This example does not require a more complex learning task in terms of the question or the data set. Rather, the complexity increases because of the expectation that the students should be including a rebuttal in their response where they refute other potential explanations.

Other Potential Variations

These are only four examples of how you could adapt the framework. There are of course multiple other possibilities as well. We see the framework as a tool that you should adapt to meet the needs of your students. For example, in working with one bilingual middle school, the teachers in the school decided to change the framework from claim, evidence, reasoning, and rebuttal (CERR) to claim, evidence, reasoning, and other explanation (CERO). They made this change for two different reasons. First, they decided to have all the middle school teachers across the content areas (math, English, social studies, and science) use the same framework. The teachers in the other content areas felt that "other explanations" were more appropriate for their content areas than the term "rebuttal." The second reason they made the change was because *cero* means "zero" in Spanish. They decided to use this to remind their students to use CERO if they did not want to get a zero for their writing. This is just one example. But the point is that there are other ways to adapt the scientific explanation framework beyond the four variations in Table 2.3. The framework is a tool for you to adapt and use to better support your students in science writing and talk.

Benefits of the Framework for All Learners

Engaging students in talking and writing scientific explanations across different science content areas can help all students achieve greater success in science as well as develop a deeper understanding of explanations and arguments that they encounter in their daily lives. Using the instructional framework can help support a variety of different students, including students with culturally and linguistically diverse backgrounds and students with special needs. In this chapter, we focus specifically on the role of the framework, while in Chapters 3 and 4 we will discuss other classroom supports and teaching strategies for supporting all students in constructing scientific explanations.

Students with Culturally and Linguistically Diverse Backgrounds

From a young age, students learn how to effectively communicate in their homes and everyday lives, yet these ways of communicating can differ compared to the academic language and academic ways of thinking that is prioritized in schools (Rosebery & Hudicourt-Barnes, 2006). Specifically, science has its own ways of knowing, talking, and writing that can be challenging for all students, particularly those from culturally and linguistically diverse backgrounds. The use of evidence, construction of explanations, and consideration and weighing of alternative explanations play key roles in science, yet they may vary from how students construct knowledge claims or create explanations in their everyday lives. Two effective strategies that can help all students are: (1) Connect students' everyday ways of knowing with scientific ways of knowing and (2) make the implicit rules of science discourse explicit (Michaels et al., 2008).

The use of evidence to support a claim can be different from how claims are supported in everyday talk. For example, some cultures prioritize storytelling as a cultural way of talking and communicating (Bransford, Brown, & Cocking, 2000).

Storytelling as a way of knowing in culture

7th graders

Constructing a story has a very different format than constructing a scientific explanation. Storytelling can prioritize communication that is more of a narrative or description and draws from experience and knowledge outside of the science context. Although storytelling is a very effective way to communicate in certain contexts, scientific explanations take on a different format. This is why it is important to understand your students' everyday meanings and uses of terms like *evidence* and *explanation*. By developing an understanding of your students' ideas about these terms and practices, you can better support them to understand how constructing explanations and using evidence are similar and different in their everyday lives compared to their lives in the science classroom.

For example, explanation may have a different connotation for students because they may think of explaining as telling a story. In Table 2.2, we discussed a physics example in which students conducted an investigation testing the effect of mass on how quickly an object falls. If students thought writing a scientific explanation about the investigation involved telling a story, they might write a more personal narrative such as, "Our group had a lot of fun testing the different blocks. We used a timer and five different blocks during our investigation." This is a very different format than stating a claim, "Mass does not affect how quickly an object falls," and then supporting that claim with evidence from the investigation. Consequently, you may need to discuss with your students how writing a scientific explanation is different from other ways of communicating, such as telling a story. In terms of evidence, students may have some initial ideas about evidence such as from television shows or movies that focus on forensic investigations. Building on these initial ideas can help students understand that "what counts" as evidence in science is different, though in both cases evidence is used to answer a question or a problem. Students' everyday knowledge can serve as a resource that can be explored and built on to enable students' greater success in constructing scientific explanations.

In addition to understanding students' prior ideas, it is also important to make the expectations of science clear to students. The scientific explanation framework makes explicit how claims are created and supported in science by breaking down this complex practice into the different components: claim, evidence, reasoning, and rebuttal. Simplifying this complex practice into the different components can help provide greater access to all students. The framework provides an entry point that allows students to better understand expectations and how to justify claims in science. Introducing and using the framework with your students can provide them with a valuable tool to enable them greater success in this complex practice.

Specifically, in terms of English language learners (ELLs) engaging in science investigations and making sense of that data through talking, listening, reading, and writing can support students in learning both science content and academic discourse. Similar to other students, ELLs need explicit support in science writing in terms of specific objectives and support to make the expectations clear and limit the complexity of the task (Maatta, Dobb, & Ostlund, 2006). Furthermore, it is important to build from their everyday knowledge and ways of knowing

(Rosebery & Hudicourt-Barnes, 2006). These recommendations align with the Sheltered Instruction Observation Protocol (SIOP) model for teaching content to English learners (Echevarria, Vogt, & Short, 2008). The SIOP model encompasses multiple recommendations for instruction, including clearly defining and displaying content and language objectives, explicitly linking concepts to students' background experiences, and using an instructional model that provides explicit teaching, modeling, and practice (Echevarria et al., 2008). Using the CER framework provides an instructional model that can be used as a tool to integrate these instructional strategies into science classrooms for ELLs and other students with culturally and linguistically diverse backgrounds.

Students with Special Needs

⟋70¹

Currently, many students with special needs are mainstreamed in general science classrooms and may have a variety of disabilities including learning disabilities, intellectual disabilities, behavioral disorders, attention deficits/hyperactivity, and language impairments (Steele, 2005). Individual accommodations and modifications need to be made for each student with special needs. The use of the instructional framework for scientific explanation is a strategy that can benefit all students. The scientific explanation framework can provide structure, repetition, and practice for a key way of knowing in science. Students with learning disabilities can have difficulty organizing what they have learned, making connections, and expressing their ideas (Steele, 2005). The claim, evidence, and reasoning structure can support students with these aspects. Furthermore, the framework breaks down this complex task into simpler components, which can help make this way of talking and writing more accessible to all students. Finally, the reasoning component highlights the important science concepts, which can help students understand the concepts as well as encourage them to apply the concepts to different contexts. As such, the scientific explanation framework provides a heuristic that can benefit all learners. In the next two chapters, we will discuss additional strategies that can be used in conjunction with the framework such as visual organizers, picture cues, and modeling to help all students succeed in constructing scientific explanations.

Check Point

At this point, we have described why scientific explanation is important for science classrooms as well as introduced a framework that you can use with your students. The components of the scientific explanation framework include: claim, evidence, reasoning, and rebuttal. The framework can be adapted to meet the needs of your particular students and it can increase in complexity over time as students develop a stronger understanding. In this chapter our goal was to describe what the framework looks like across science content areas and illustrate what it might look like to introduce the framework to your students. At this point, you should hopefully feel like you have a general understanding of the scientific explanation framework. In future chapters, we will describe how to integrate this framework into your classroom in order to support students in constructing scientific explanations in both writing and in classroom discussions. We will focus on how to design and use learning and assessment tasks as well as different teaching strategies you can use to support all students in this complex scientific practice.

Study Group Questions

1. Look at Table 2.3. What variation of the framework would you use in your classroom? Why? Do you think the variation you will use will change over the course of the school year? Why or why not?
2. Describe how you will introduce the scientific explanation framework to your students. Watch the video of Ms. Nelson's classroom again. How would your introduction be similar and different from how Ms. Nelson introduced the framework to her seventh-grade students?
3. Introduce the scientific explanation framework to your students (consider videotaping the introduction and then watching the lesson). What worked well? What challenges did you face? How would you introduce the framework differently next time?

Designing Learning Tasks for Your Science Curriculum

How can you design your classroom to provide students with opportunities to construct scientific explanations? How can you identify opportunities in your current science curriculum for students to construct scientific explanations? What kind of supports can you provide so that all students can take part in this complex practice? Let's consider the following vignette from Ms. Cooney's fifth-grade classroom.

Imagine a fifth-grade teacher, Ms. Cooney, planning a lesson that focuses on the survival of animals and the environment in which they live. She is working at home on the weekend planning her next week's lesson in science. Scattered in front of Ms. Cooney are her district's curriculum frameworks, the national science education standards, and the textbook adopted by her school district.

Ms. Cooney starts by carefully reading the standard from Benchmarks for Science Literacy (AAAS, 2008) she wants her students to learn:

> *For any particular environment, some kinds of plants and animals thrive, some do not live as well, and some do not survive at all. (5D/E1, AAAS, 2008)*

She also considers the five essential features of classroom inquiry (NRC, 2000):

1. *Learner engages in scientifically oriented questions*
2. *Learner gives priority to evidence in responding to questions*
3. *Learner formulates explanations from evidence*
4. *Learner connects explanations to scientific knowledge*
5. *Learner communicates and justifies explanations*

Taking into consideration the content standard, the essential features of classroom inquiry and the focus of her curriculum on using local ecosystems, Ms. Cooney plans her lesson. She begins by writing the following learning goal for her students. In writing her learning goal, Ms. Cooney also reflects on the importance of breaking down the task of writing an explanation into three components of claim, evidence, and reasoning that she learned at a schoolwide workshop on science teaching:

> *Students will construct a scientific explanation stating a claim about the type of animals that survive in the local environment, providing evidence for the characteristics of animals and characteristics of the environment, and reasoning about why the environment is favorable for these types of animals to survive.*

Ms. Cooney decides that to meet this learning goal, she will engage her students in answering the following questions: What types of animals live around our playground and why are they able to survive in this environment? She also decides that she will take her students outside during science period to observe the animals and the environment. In order to support her students in making observations, she designs a worksheet to support their data collection that includes three columns: (1) animal identity, (2) characteristics of animal that help it survive, and (3) characteristics of environment that the animal uses. Finally, she thinks it is essential to present her students with the major task of the lesson—constructing a scientific explanation. Although Ms. Cooney has introduced her students to scientific explanations in the previous unit on forces and motion, she decides it is still important to support her students in the process. She designs the following handout.

> Construct a scientific explanation that answers the following
> questions: What types of animals live around our playground
> and why are they able to survive in this environment?
>
> Remember a scientific explanation includes a claim, evidence,
> and reasoning.
> • Claim: a statement that answers the question
> • Evidence: scientific data that supports the claim (remember
>   the evidence needs to be both sufficient and appropriate)
> • Reasoning: a justification for why the evidence supports the
>   claim using scientific principles

*Ms. Cooney is pleased with this task because it aligns well with her goals
for her students and she believes it will engage her students.*

This scenario illustrates how a fifth-grade teacher plans a lesson to support
students in constructing scientific explanations. In planning her lesson, Ms. Cooney
took into consideration the content standard she hopes students will learn and the
national science education standards on inquiry. Furthermore, she adapted her current science curriculum so that the lesson fit well into the overarching sequence of
the unit. She also realized that her students still needed support in constructing an
explanation even though she introduced scientific explanation in a previous unit.

In this chapter, we explore how you can design learning tasks and classroom support to help your students in constructing scientific explanations. This process begins
by identifying places in your curriculum that provide opportunities for scientific
explanations. We also examine how you can design the learning tasks with varying
degrees of complexity to meet the needs of all your students. Finally, we discuss how
you can develop classroom supports, such as visual representations and scaffolds, that
aid students in this complex practice. With appropriate support, all students can succeed in this important scientific inquiry practice that is essential for scientific literacy.

Considerations for Designing Learning Tasks

Designing or adapting existing readings, activities, and investigations in your science
curriculum in order to provide students with opportunities to engage in scientific
explanation can pose challenges for practicing teachers. The particular learning task
needs to be appropriate for the use of the claim, evidence, and reasoning framework;
furthermore, you want to provide your students with the appropriate amount of support so that all your students will be successful. When we design learning tasks we
engage in three overarching steps: (1) Identify Opportunities in the Curriculum,
(2) Design Complexity of the Learning Task, and (3) Create Classroom Supports.

TABLE 3.1 Considerations for Designing Learning Tasks

Step 1: Identify Opportunities in the Curriculum
    1a. Learning Goal
    1b. Scientific Data
    1c. Scientific Principle

Step 2: Design Complexity of the Learning Task
    2a. Openness of Question
    2b. Type of Data
    2c. Amount of Data
    2d. Inclusion of Rebuttal

Step 3: Create Classroom Supports
    3a. Visual Representations
    3b. Curricular Scaffolds

Each step includes multiple parts (see Table 3.1), which we will discuss in more detail as well as provide examples to illustrate both what is and what is not an effective learning task to support students in scientific explanation.

Step 1: Identify Opportunities in the Curriculum

The first step is to identify opportunities in your curriculum where it makes sense to ask students to construct a scientific explanation. In determining the appropriateness of a particular reading, activity, or investigation, it is important to consider three key features: (1) the learning goal or learning performance, (2) whether the task includes students analyzing data, and (3) whether the task requires students to apply or develop scientific principles. Keeping these three features in mind will allow you to design scientific explanation learning tasks that provide students with the opportunity to construct a response in which they justify their claim with appropriate evidence and reasoning.

Learning Goal

We often ask students to write or have discussions in science class. There are many times when the goal of that learning task is to have students construct and justify a claim. Yet many other important science learning tasks do not align with the scientific explanation framework. For example, you might ask students to define the word force or give an everyday example of a *force* they experienced that morning. Both of these are great questions to determine if students understand a concept. The first question provides a sense of whether your students can define a force as a push or a pull and the second question offers whether they can identify forces around them. The goals of these questions are different from asking students to construct a scientific explanation where they would apply their understanding of force to make sense of data and construct an appropriate claim. When designing a learning task, it is important to consider the goal of the task. You want to consider what it is that you want students to be able to "do" with their science knowledge and whether or not that goal aligns with the scientific explanation framework.

When we develop learning goals for science classrooms, we call them learning performances. A learning performance combines both the science content and the scientific inquiry practice to specify what students should be able to do with the content (Krajcik, McNeill, & Reiser, 2008; McNeill & Krajcik, 2008b). A learning performance goes beyond just stating a definition of the key science concept (e.g., a force is a push or a pull) to articulating how students should apply or use the content knowledge. Figure 3.1 provides an example of a learning performance focused on the content of forces and motion and the scientific inquiry practice of scientific explanation.

The example in Figure 3.1 illustrates how the content was combined with the claim, evidence, and reasoning framework to specify a learning performance for the students. The learning performance specifies what the claim, evidence, and reasoning look like for this force-and-motion content. Learning performances can also be developed for other scientific inquiry practices, such as designing an investigation or constructing a model. In all cases, they specify what you would like students to be able to do with the content in terms of a specific performance. The main point of mentioning learning performances here is to stress the importance of considering the learning goal when you design new tasks or adapt tasks in your current science curriculum to provide students with an opportunity to construct scientific explanations. You need to consider your learning goal for the students as well as other features of the learning task to determine if this is an appropriate opportunity for

---

FIGURE 3.1

Developing Learning Performances

Content Standard ×	Scientific Inquiry = Standard	Learning Performance
The position and motion of objects can be changed by pushing or pulling. The size of the change is related to the strength of the push or pull. (NRC, 1996, B: 2/3, 5–8)	Develop . . . explanations . . . using evidence. (NRC, 1996, A: 1/4, 5–8) Think critically and logically to make the relationships between evidence and explanation. (NRC, 1996, A: 1/5, 5–8)	Students construct a scientific explanation that includes a claim about how the size of a force impacts the position of an object, evidence in the form of different forces and the related distance that an object traveled, and reasoning that a force is a push or a pull and that the larger the force the greater the distance an object will travel.

scientific explanation. Every lesson will not be appropriate for students to construct a scientific explanation; rather, you may ask students to engage in scientific explanation once a week or once a month when the activities or investigations in class include the three important features.

Scientific Data

In order for students to construct a scientific explanation in writing or in a classroom discussion, the learning task must include data and require students to make sense of that data. Since science is fundamentally about explaining the world around us and using evidence to support those explanations, students need to have data to analyze and consider as evidence. The data can either be collected by the student as part of an investigation or the data can be provided to students such as a data table, text, or database. For example, to return to the force example mentioned earlier in this chapter, students could be answering the question: How does the size of a force affect how far a car travels? To construct a scientific explanation to answer this question, students might collect data by doing an investigation where they apply different size forces to a car and then measure how far the car travels. In this case, they would be analyzing data they collected themselves. Another possibility is that the teacher gives students a data table with information indicating how far a car travels when different size forces are applied, which they need to analyze to answer the question. In either case, students have some data that they may use as evidence to support their answer to the question about the effect of force on how far a car travels.

Sometimes in science class we discuss science topics that students cannot directly explore, because the topic in question occurred a long time ago (e.g., dinosaur extinction), over a period of time too long to directly observe (e.g., evolution), on too large of a scale (e.g., rotation of the earth), or on too small of a scale (e.g., particulate nature of matter). These topics can still provide opportunities for scientific explanation, but they necessitate that students analyze data that is provided for them. For example, students can examine the question: Why did the dinosaurs go extinct? In answering this question, students read text and identify evidence scientists have used to support their claims about potential causes of the extinction or they research evidence online or in the library. Then students use the claim, evidence, reasoning, and rebuttal framework to write a scientific explanation or engage in debate about the cause of the dinosaur extinction.

Engaging in scientific explanation requires identifying instances in the existing curriculum or designing activities when students are making sense of data. Students do not need to collect the data themselves, but there does need to be data they can use as evidence to support their claim.

Scientific Principles

Another important feature of the learning task is that it aligns with a scientific principle. The National Research Council (2000) describes how scientific inquiry practices, such as constructing a scientific explanation, are intimately intermingled with the science concepts. Scientific inquiry learning tasks should not be content free, but rather, must require students to use science principles to answer important questions and make sense of the world around them. The reasoning component of the scientific explanation framework explicitly asks students to use science principles to provide their rationale for why their evidence supports their claim. Constructing scientific explanations provides students with practice using science principles they already learned and supports them in developing understandings of new principles. For example, with the previous question, How does the size of a force affect how far a car travels? students need to apply their understanding of a force as a push or a pull to answer the question. Furthermore, by analyzing the data and constructing a scientific explanation they expand their conceptual understanding to include the idea that the larger a force, the farther an object will travel. In order to answer the question, Why did the dinosaurs go extinct? students need to apply their understanding of needs of living things for survival and potential causes of extinction. When they examine the data collected by scientists, they use their understandings of these science concepts to construct or justify their own claim about the cause of the dinosaur extinction.

When identifying opportunities in your current curriculum where students could construct scientific explanations or when designing new scientific explanation learning tasks, you want to keep these three characteristics in mind. You need to consider the learning goal of the task and whether or not you want students to construct a scientific explanation or engage in another practice such as defining or designing an experiment. You want to identify or create opportunities for students to analyze data that they have either collected themselves or been given. You also want to keep in mind what scientific principles students use or develop by answering the particular question.

Examples of Learning Tasks

To illustrate these three important features for identifying opportunities in the curriculum, we discuss a variety of learning tasks that both are and are not appropriate for asking students to use the scientific explanation framework. These examples come from different science topics, because students can construct scientific explanations across physics, chemistry, biology, and earth science. Regardless of the science content area, you want to consider the learning goal, whether the task includes data, and whether the task requires the use of scientific principles to determine if the task is an appropriate area to ask students to construct a scientific explanation. Table 3.2 lists examples of questions for specific science content that provide students with opportunities to construct a scientific explanation as well as examples of other scientific learning tasks to illustrate the difference.

TABLE 3.2 Examples of Scientific Learning Tasks

Content Area	Scientific Explanation Learning Tasks	Other Scientific Learning Tasks (e.g., define, identify, compare)
Physics • Force and Motion	How does the size of a force affect how far a car travels?	• Define the word *force*. • Provide an everyday example of a force.
Physics • Simple Machines	What type of pulley system requires the least force to move the block?	• Describe the different pulley systems. • Draw a picture comparing two different pulley systems.
Chemistry • States of Matter	Is the unknown a solid, a liquid, or a gas?	• Define solid, liquid, and gas. • Provide examples of a solid, liquid, and gas.
Chemistry • Conservation of Mass	What happens to the mass of a system during a chemical reaction?	• Define *conservation of mass*. • Design an experiment that would test whether mass is conserved.
Biology • Characteristics of Living Things	Is a seed a living thing?	• Describe the characteristics of living things. • Compare how living and nonliving things are similar and different.
Biology • Human Body and Cells	What activity (sitting, walking, jumping jacks) requires the most nutrients and oxygen for the cells in our body?	• Describe how the digestive, circulatory, and respiratory system work together to provide cells with nutrients and oxygen. • Draw a picture of the human body that illustrates the pathway of nutrients and oxygen.
Earth Science • Rocks and Minerals	What type of mineral is this sample?	• List three different minerals. • Describe the properties that allow you to identify minerals.
Earth Science • Continental Drift	Did the land on earth start off as one giant continent?	• Describe the theory of continental drift. • Compare maps of the continents for the last 200 years showing how the continent moved.

Scientific Explanation Learning Tasks

All eight of the questions in Table 3.2 for the scientific explanation learning tasks require students to use data and scientific principles to formulate a claim. The type of the data varies as well as whether the students would be able to collect the data themselves or if it would need to be provided to them. We discuss four of the eight examples in more detail, describing what the evidence and scientific principle would look like.

Fifth-grade Physics Example. The physics question focused on simple machines asks: What type of pulley system requires the least force to move the block? Fifth-grade students conduct an investigation where they design different pulley systems, using both fixed and moveable pulleys, to move a 300-gram block. They conduct three trials for each pulley system and calculate the average Newtons for each pulley system. Then the students compare the quantitative data for the different simple machines and apply their scientific understandings of different types of pulley systems and force. One group writes a scientific explanation where they state a claim: *A pulley system with two moveable pulleys and one fixed pulley required the least amount of force to move the block.* The fifth-graders justify their claim by using the data from their investigation: *This system took an average of 0.82 Newtons to move the block. We tried three other systems, but the closest one was still 0.23 Newtons more, because it required 1.05 Newtons.* In their reasoning, the students then apply their understanding of pulleys: *The fixed pulleys just change the direction of the force, while moveable pulleys reduce the amount of force. Using one fixed allowed us to have two moveable pulleys, which decreased the force more than just having one moveable pulley.* The reasoning explains the students' logic for why their pulley system was most effective at reducing the force. Including the reasoning encourages students to reflect on the science concepts and how they used them to make sense of their data.

Seventh-grade Chemistry Example. For the chemistry question about conservation of mass, seventh-grade students investigate: What happens to the mass of a system during a chemical reaction? The students had studied chemical reactions and understood that a chemical reaction results in a new substance with new properties. The students disagreed whether the new substance resulted from a rearrangement of the old substances or if the new substance just appeared and was totally new and not created from the old substances. Consequently, their teacher asked them to investigate whether the mass of the old substances was the same or different compared to the new substances. The students collect quantitative data of the mass of baking soda and vinegar before combining the two substances. Then they combine the two substances in a soda bottle with the top on, observe the chemical reaction, and find the mass of the new substances in the soda bottle. Finally, they take the top off the soda bottle and release the gas to find out the mass of the open system when the gas is released. The students then write the following scientific explanation:

> *Mass stayed the same when baking soda reacted with vinegar in a closed system (CLAIM). With the top on, the total mass before the reaction was 154.1 g, and the total mass after the reaction was 154.1 g. When we took the top off the bottle, the mass decreased by 2.1 g (EVIDENCE). We put a top on the bottle so we were able to trap all the gas of the reaction. Since the reaction occurred in a closed system, nothing could leave or enter the system and the mass stayed the same. In a chemical reaction material is neither created nor destroyed. This is why the mass stays the same (REASONING).*

The seventh-graders justify their claim using the evidence from their investigation as well as expand their understanding of chemical reaction and conservation of mass in their reasoning. This task is appropriate to ask students to construct a scientific explanation because they are using science concepts to make sense of data they collected.

Sixth-grade Biology Example. The biology example about characteristics of living things asks sixth-grade students to answer the question: Is a seed a living thing? As a class, the students and their teacher develop a list of six characteristics of living things: they are made of cells, obtain and use energy, grow and develop, reproduce, respond to their environment, and adapt to their environment. The teacher then breaks the students into six groups and each group is responsible for one of the six characteristics. Each group must either conduct an experiment or do research to find evidence for whether or not a seed has that characteristic of a living thing. For example, the group that receives "grow and develop," plants some seeds in soil to investigate whether the seeds will grow, while the group that receives "adapt to their environment," conducts research online to explore how seeds have changed over time to different environments. The groups post their evidence on large paper at the front of the room and as a class they construct a scientific explanation. The class agrees on the claim: *A seed is a living thing.* They also agree on their reasoning that in order to be classified as living something needs to have all six characteristics. Each group then provides evidence for their investigation of a particular characteristic. Engaging in this full-class exploration supports the students in developing a deeper understanding of the characteristics of living things by applying them to a real-life example.

Eighth-grade Earth Science Example. Finally, the earth science example about continental drift asks students: Did the land on earth start off as one giant continent? In this example, the eighth-grade students are unable to conduct experiments in class to collect data to address this question since this phenomenon occurred millions of years ago. Instead, students rotate through different stations that include readings and activities where they obtain evidence scientists have collected to investigate this question, such as the shapes of the continents, the types of plant and animal fossils found on the different continents, and the types of rocks found on the different continents. The eighth-grade students then apply their understandings of plate tectonics and the movement of the earth's crust to make sense of the evidence. The students write the following scientific explanation:

> *The land on earth started as one giant continent (CLAIM). The shapes of the different continents fit together into one, like a puzzle. Fossils from identical plant and animal species and rocks of the same age and type have been found on adjacent continents. There is also evidence of ancient mountain chains and glacial scratches that match up the different adjacent continents (EVIDENCE). Since the earth is made up of different tectonic*

plates that change shape and position over time, this suggest that the continents have not always been in their current locations. The pattern of evidence from the different continents suggests they were all once joined together as a super continent.

Although the students are unable to collect the data themselves, they are still able to consider and use the data scientists have collected to address this historical scientific question. Examining the evidence allows them to develop a stronger understanding of this important scientific concept.

Each of the eight different scientific explanation learning tasks listed in Table 3.2 shares in common the three key features: a learning goal focused on constructing a scientific explanation, the analysis of data to answer the question, and the application or development of scientific principles. When the task has these characteristics, students can construct a response either in talk or writing that corresponds with the scientific explanation framework of claim, evidence, and reasoning. As you are identifying places in your current science curriculum to add scientific explanations, you should look for these features. Each of these learning tasks allows learners in grades 5 through 8 to develop important skills related to the use of evidence and communication that they can use not only in science, but throughout their lives.

Other Scientific Learning Tasks

As we mentioned previously, there are many other scientific learning tasks that are valuable for students to engage in, but do not provide students with opportunities to create scientific explanations. We want to discuss this point in more detail, because it has been unclear for some individuals we have worked with in the past. We ask students to engage in a variety of different activities in science class that do not require that students make sense of data using scientific principles. For example, we can ask students to engage in tasks such as defining, identifying, classifying, comparing, describing, and providing an example. These are all important objectives to help students develop understandings of science concepts, but you would not expect a student's response to include a claim justified with evidence and reasoning. Furthermore, you can ask students to complete these different learning tasks for the same science content goals, but the learning performance looks different. No longer does the learning performance include the structure of claim, evidence, and reasoning; rather, the learning performance includes another action such as defining or creating a model. Column three in Table 3.2 provides other scientific learning tasks for the same content goals for which we previously discussed scientific explanation learning tasks. For example, in teaching students about simple machines you might ask students to describe different pulley systems or draw a picture comparing different pulley systems. A student might describe a simple class 1 pulley system as consisting of one pulley that is fixed or attached to a surface that changes the direction of the force, but not does change the amount of the force. This is an excellent response to this question, but the response does not include evidence to support a claim because the student is not analyzing and making sense of data. The student is stating a scientific principle about pulleys, but not applying that principle to construct a scientific explanation.

If you ask students to justify a claim with evidence and reasoning for a learning task that does not include the important features, you may confuse students about the meanings of the three terms. For example, one teacher we worked with provided her students with the following learning task: *Write a scientific explanation about three everyday examples of chemical reactions.* The students were asked to write the scientific explanation in class without conducting investigations to collect data, being provided data, or doing research to find data. Without data, many of the students struggled to have their writing align with the framework of claim, evidence, and reasoning because they did not have any evidence for the claims that they made. Although this is a great question to help students connect chemical reactions to their everyday lives, it is not an appropriate learning task for the scientific explanation framework. Such a task confuses students about what counts as evidence and what the difference is between evidence and reasoning. Consequently, it is important to limit asking students to use the framework in their responses to situations that include the use of data and scientific principles.

Students need to practice constructing scientific explanations in order to become more proficient at justifying their claims with evidence and reasoning. But you will not have your students construct new scientific explanations during every science class. Rather, this may be a learning task you have students engage in once a week or once a month when they are trying to make sense of data using scientific principles. It is important to carefully design these experiences so that students have an opportunity to deepen their understanding of scientific explanations, demonstrate their ability to engage in this important scientific practice, and develop important skills such as problem solving by using evidence and communication.

Step 2: Design Complexity of the Learning Task

After identifying appropriate places in your curriculum to integrate scientific explanations, you then need to design the actual learning tasks. In designing learning tasks, there are a number of different choices you can make to modify the complexity of the task to meet the needs of your students. Table 3.3 lists some of the characteristics of learning tasks that influence the complexity or difficulty of the task for students. We also include two different variations of a learning task focused on the needs of plants for survival to illustrate how you can alter the complexity by changing various characteristics. The two variations both focus on the needs of plants, but the more complex task is more challenging for students in terms of constructing an appropriate claim, making sense of the data, using more complex scientific principles, and providing a rebuttal for alternative explanations. Developing different

TABLE 3.3 Characteristics of Learning Tasks that Impact Complexity

Characteristic	Simple Task	Complex Task
Openness of Question	• Does providing a plant with light 12 hours a day or 24 hours a day impact the growth of a plant?	• What factors impact the growth of a plant?
Type of Data	• Height in cm of plants	• Height in cm of plants • Number of leaves, buds, and flowers • Description of leaves, buds, and flowers to indicate health
Amount of Data	• 3 plants in 2 conditions (6 total plants) • Measured once a week for 4 weeks (24 total height measurements)	• 3 plants each in 8 different conditions to investigate 3 different variables (24 total plants) • Measured once a week for 8 weeks (192 measurements or observations for each type of data)
Inclusion of Rebuttal	• Not asked to provide an alternative explanation	• Asked to provide an alternative claim and why it is not the correct response to the question

variations of the same tasks can allow you to modify a task so all students can take part in constructing scientific explanations and develop their skills of problem solving using reasoning and communication.

Openness of Question

The first characteristic to consider is the openness of the question. A question can be phrased so that students have a limited number of possible claims and data to collect to answer the question. If you think your students will have difficulty coming up with different claims or determining appropriate claims, you can limit the openness of the question. For example, younger or inexperienced students can struggle with constructing a claim that answers the question. Their claim can be related to the question, but not directly answer the question. In this case, it is important to narrow the number of claims students can make to directly answer the question. For example, the simple task in Table 3.3 asks: Does providing a plant with light 12 hours a day or 24 hours a day result in a taller plant? The phrasing of the question limits the claim to two different possibilities—12 hours or 24 hours. More experienced students may not struggle with creating claims so you can provide a more open-ended question to push students to apply their understandings of both scientific explanations and the science content. The more complex task in Table 3.3 asks: What factors impact the growth of a plant? This question is open in that students could discuss a variety of different factors that impact a plant's growth in their claim, such as light, water, nutrients, space, air, and pollution. In both tasks, students investigate what influences plant growth, but the complexity of the two questions is different.

Characteristics of Data

Another way to influence the complexity of the task is by changing the data students use to answer the question. You can alter the complexity of the data by changing either the type of data or amount of data. These two characteristics can be related in that a larger data set may include a larger variety of types of data, but you can also change one characteristic of the data without altering the other.

Type of Data. There are multiple types of data that students can use to construct a scientific explanation. Typically, it is easier for students to focus on one type of data. Furthermore, it can also be easier for students to use quantitative data as evidence, because they more easily recognize numbers as data. Qualitative data, such as observations, can be less intuitive for students to think of as data and can be harder for them to observe patterns or trends. Consequently, having different types of data makes the scientific explanation task more difficult. For example, in Table 3.3 the simple task only includes the height of the plants in centimeters, while the complex task includes multiple different types of data including both quantitative (e.g., height and number of leaves, buds, and flowers) and qualitative data (description of leaves, buds, and flowers to indicate health). Having more types of data makes answering the question more complex, because the different types of data may contradict each other. For example, the tallest plant could have fewer leaves, no flowers, and appear yellowish in color while a shorter plant could have numerous leaves, numerous flowers, and be vibrant green. In this case, the students have to decide which plant they consider as having more growth.

Amount of Data. Besides varying the types of data, you can also alter the task to change the amount of data that students collect or that is provided to them. For example, the simple task limits students to two different conditions, and they collect data for 4 weeks for a total of 24 data points. In the more complex task, students collect data in eight different conditions in order to investigate three different variables—such as 12 hours versus 24 hours of light, 20 mL of water versus 40 mL of water, and 1 fertilizer tablet versus 2 fertilizer tablets. Furthermore, the students collect data for a longer amount of time, which results in 192 measurements or observations for each type of data. Consequently, the more complex example includes more data for a couple of different reasons—more conditions, more time points, and more types of data. Although we only present two different examples here, the scientific explanation learning task has a range of complexity depending on how you structure the data students collect or the complexity of the data you provide to students to analyze. Scientific explanation learning tasks do not need to be either simple or complex, but rather can be designed along a continuum. As your students gain experience, you want to move them along this continuum to support them in developing more complex problem-solving skills.

The complexity of the question and the data impacts the complexity of the reasoning your students provide as part of the scientific explanation, but it is not a separate characteristic that you can alter independent of these other characteristics. Rather, the phrasing of the question and the complexity of the data determine the complexity of the reasoning. For example, the reasoning in the simple task only requires a simple discussion of the effect of light on plants, such as: *Plants require light to grow and develop. This is why the plant that received 24 hours of light grew taller.* For the more complex task, the student's reasoning includes a discussion of the science behind how all the different variables (e.g., light, water, and carbon dioxide) impact plant growth. For example, a student provides a more complex discussion of photosynthesis: *Photosynthesis is the process where green plants produce sugar from water, carbon dioxide, and light energy. Producing sugar is essential for plant growth and development. That is why the plants that received a constant source of water, carbon dioxide, and light grew the most.* Consequently, reasoning is not included in Table 3.3 as a characteristic of the learning task that you will alter. Rather, your other choices in designing the task determine the complexity of the reasoning.

Inclusion of Rebuttal

In designing a scientific explanation learning task, you must also decide whether or not to ask your students to provide a rebuttal. The simple task does not ask students to provide a rebuttal. Rather, their scientific explanation consists only of a claim, evidence, and reasoning similar to Variation #1 of the scientific explanation framework we discussed in Chapter 2 (see Table 2.3). In the more complex task, students include a rebuttal that discusses an alternative explanation for the data and why they believe it is not the correct response to the question. Deciding whether or not to ask for a rebuttal will depend on your students' level of proficiency with constructing scientific explanations. Including a rebuttal increases the complexity of the task, because it requires students to consider the question from multiple perspectives.

Although Table 3.3 shows that the complex task includes greater complexity for all four different characteristics, in actuality you can design the task to include some simpler characteristics and other more complex characteristics. For example, you could present your students with the more open and complex question: What factors impact the growth of a plant? But your directions for them to design their investigation would include that they need to choose one variable to study (e.g., fertilizer) and that they will be collecting data once a week for 4 weeks. This example includes a more complex question, which would require them to think about their claim and consider what factors they believe impact plant growth. But the task also limits their data collection, which would aid them in providing evidence to support their claim. Another example would be to provide your students with an intermediate question: How does light impact the growth of plants? Then provide them with an intermediate data set that includes both quantitative and qualitative data. There is considerable flexibility in how you can design a scientific explanation learning task to vary the complexity to meet the needs of all students. As students gain experience with constructing scientific explanations, you can increase the complexity thereby engaging students in more complex scientific thinking.

Step 3: Create Classroom Support

Besides changing the learning task in terms of its characteristics, such as the type of question or the amount of available data, another way to change the complexity is by altering the instructional support you provide students. One way to provide support to your students is by developing and using scaffolds. Scaffolds are temporary supports provided by the teacher, curriculum, technology, or other tools that promote student learning of complex problem solving (Bransford et al., 2000). The amount of support provided by the scaffold should decrease over time. The ultimate goal is that eventually when you remove the scaffold your students will independently reach the same high level of achievement on the learning task. Yet when students are new at constructing scientific explanations, are struggling with particular aspects of scientific explanations, or are creating them in a new content area, this type of support can help them achieve greater success than they could achieve on their own.

Designing scaffolds can allow all learners to successfully take part in this practice, including students with culturally and linguistically diverse backgrounds and special needs. For example, the SIOP model advocates the use of visual aids, graphic organizers, and other types of scaffolding in developing instructional support for English learners in the core subject areas, including science (Echevarria, Vogt, & Short, 2008). Scaffolds can help provide reminders and simplify this complex task to make it accessible to all your students. Depending on the students in your classroom, you may also decide to design individualized scaffolds for specific students. This individualized support is one strategy to differentiate your instruction to meet the needs of specific learners in your classroom.

In this chapter, we specifically focus on scaffolds that you can design ahead of the lessons: visual representations and curricular scaffolds (see Table 3.4). Teachers may also provide scaffolding during instruction through the use of different instructional strategies such as asking questions, providing feedback, and modeling. Chapter 4 will specifically focus on these and other teaching strategies you can incorporate into your classroom when you are working with your students.

Visual Representation

When you first introduce the scientific explanation framework to your students, they may have difficulty remembering the different components. Creating and posting a

TABLE 3.4 Two Types of Scaffolds to Support Students in Scientific Explanation

Scaffold Type	Example
Visual Representation	Poster on the wall of the classroom titled "Scientific Explanation" with claim, evidence, and reasoning listed underneath and the definition of each component.
Curricular Scaffolds	Sentence starters, prompts, or questions included on an investigation sheet to remind and provide students with support around including claim, evidence, and reasoning in their written response.

visual representation or reminder on the classroom wall helps to support their understanding of the framework. For example, Figure 3.2 shows such a visual support similar to the one created and posted by Ms. Hill on the wall in her seventh-grade classroom at the beginning of the school year. This constant reminder encouraged Ms. Hill's students to include claim, evidence, and reasoning both in their writing and classroom discussions when they were making sense of data and justifying claims.

Once they remember the components, students often still struggle with what each of the components means (e.g., What is the difference between evidence and reasoning?) or what that component looks like in a particular content area (e.g., What is evidence of biodiversity?). You can develop a more detailed visual reminder than

FIGURE 3.2

Scientific Explanation Visual

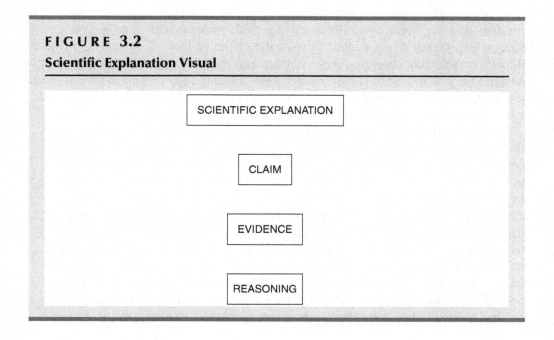

Figure 3.2 by adding other features such as definitions, examples, or nonexamples for each component. For example, next to each component you could include a definition such as: *A claim is a conclusion for a question or problem.* You may also want to include an image next to each component, such as a magnifying glass next to evidence, to provide a pictorial reminder. Another way to represent the framework would be as a diagram, such as Figure 2.1 or Figure 2.2 in Chapter 2, that uses arrows to show the relationships between the different components.

Over the course of the school year, you can change or add to the visual representation depending on the content of your current curriculum or if the level of complexity you expect from your students increases. For example, you could include an example of each component in the representation during a unit on ecosystems. Then when you start a new unit, such as one on simple machines, you could revisit the visual and add new examples from the physical science content. This can help students see how the same framework can be used across different science content. Another example would be to start with claim, evidence, and reasoning at the beginning of the school year, then toward the end of the school year add the rebuttal component to the visual. You could introduce the idea of including alternative explanations and begin requiring that aspect after students have become more comfortable with the other three components.

Curricular Scaffolds

Curricular scaffolds can be designed for each investigation or activity to support students in constructing more thorough and accurate scientific explanations. Curricular scaffolds are sentence starters, subquestions, graphic organizers, or prompts that help break down the task and provide students with hints on how to successfully complete the scientific explanation learning task. These can be included directly on a student sheet or, if your students use science journals, you can project or write the prompts on the board and have the students copy them into their science journals. You can design curricular scaffolds for all the students in your class or you can design individualized scaffolds to meet the needs of specific students.

Mr. Cardone developed curricular scaffolds for his fifth-grade students during their ecosystem unit. The students built ecocolumns that included both terrestrial organisms (e.g., grass and pill bugs) and aquatic organisms (e.g., elodea and fish) in 2-liter soda bottles. Over a one-month period, the students recorded observations of their ecocolumns in their science journals to investigate how the ecosystems changed. At the beginning of the school year, Mr. Cardone introduced his class to the claim, evidence, and reasoning framework, which he referred to as a "scientific argument." For this learning task, he provided his students with the following writing prompt: *Write an argument that answers the question: Is my ecocolumn a stable ecosystem?* From earlier writing tasks, Mr. Cardone found that his students needed more structure or scaffolding in their writing. The majority of the students in Mr. Cardone's class were English language learners (ELLs) and many of them

struggled with science writing. Consequently, he designed prompts on the students'
investigation sheets to remind them of the different components, and he defined the
components and provided them with support specifically related to the ecocolumn
task. Figure 3.3 is an example of both the curricular scaffolds and the writing from
one student, Carlos, who was born in El Salvador and moved to the United States
with his family when he was five years old. At home, Carlos only spoke in Spanish
with his family. Consequently, his experiences with English occurred predominately

---

FIGURE 3.3

Curricular Scaffolds for Ecocolumn Learning Task

Write an argument that answers the question: Is my ecocolumn a stable ecosystem?

Claim
(Write a sentence stating whether your ecocolumn is or is not stable.)

I think that is not stable.

Evidence
(Provide scientific data to support your claim. Use evidence from your table above
about the health and changes for the different characteristics of your ecocolumn.)

because they don't more and
because the wrate is not clenn.
and because the plct are
not grewing.

Reasoning
(Explain why your evidence supports your claim. Describe what it means for an
ecosystem to be stable and why your evidence allowed you to determine if your
ecocolumn was stable.)

the I Know that a stable
eco- colamn has living plants
and animls. my evdence show
that there arend living pants or
animals. that is why eco column
is unstable.

in the school setting. Although he struggled with his writing (e.g., wrate = water and plot = plant), he was still able to construct a claim, use data from his observations, and articulate his reasoning using what he knows about stable ecosystems.

The example in Figure 3.3 from Carlos is very different from his science writing at the beginning of the year. The first time in the school year that Mr. Cardone asked Carlos to write a scientific argument, Carlos wrote nothing down on his paper. Now, using the structure of claim, evidence, and reasoning as well as the scaffolds on the student sheet, Carlos was offered guidance in his writing by having a stronger sense of Mr. Cardone's expectations. Using both the overarching framework and curricular scaffolds helped Mr. Cardone's students to produce stronger science writing.

General versus Content-specific Scaffolds. In developing curricular scaffolds for student sheets, it can be helpful to think about the type of language to use in the scaffolds. Specifically, we consider both *general* and *content-specific* support in the scaffolds we develop for students. Table 3.5 provides examples of two different curricular scaffolds we used with seventh-grade students during a chemistry unit (McNeill & Krajcik, 2009). The students completed an investigation in which they combined a variety of different substances in a plastic bag. They were then asked to write a response to the following prompt: *Write a scientific explanation that states whether a chemical reaction occurred in the plastic bag experiment.*

TABLE 3.5 Content-specific versus Generic Explanation Scaffolds

Content-specific Scaffold	Generic Explanation Scaffold
(State whether a chemical reaction occurred in the plastic bag experiment, that is, whether it created new substances. Provide a change in properties, such as melting point, solubility, and density, to support whether or not the experiment was a chemical reaction. Do not include measurements that are not properties, such as mass and volume. Tell why properties staying the same or changing tells you whether a chemical reaction occurred.)	**Claim** (Write a statement that responds to the original problem.) **Evidence** (Provide scientific data to support your claim. You should only use appropriate data and include enough data. Appropriate data is relevant for the problem and allows you to figure out your claim. Remember that not all data is appropriate. Enough data refers to providing the pieces of data necessary to convince someone of your claim.) **Reasoning** (In your reasoning statement, connect your claim and evidence to show how your data links to your claim. Also, tell why your data count as evidence to support your claim by using scientific principles. Remember, reasoning is the process where you apply your science knowledge to solve a problem.)

Content-specific scaffolds provide support that is specific to the content and the task students are trying to answer. General scaffolds provide support for the scientific explanation framework that could be used in any content area. For example, in Table 3.5 the content-specific scaffold reminds students that they should be using melting point, solubility, and density to determine whether a chemical reaction has occurred and not mass or volume. This prompt is telling the students what type of evidence they should be using, though it does not use the general term evidence. Instead, the prompt focuses on the specific content and task. The generic explanation scaffold in Table 3.5 provides general support that could be used in any science content. For example, the prompt provides a definition of evidence that states, "Provide scientific data to support your claim. You should only use appropriate data and include enough data." From our research, we found that when students were provided with both content-specific and general support through the variety of scaffolds incorporated in the classroom, students had the greatest learning gains in terms of their ability to justify their claims with appropriate evidence and reasoning (McNeill & Krajcik, 2009). Students need to develop an understanding of the framework as well as how to use the framework in different science content areas.

In Mr. Cardone's prompts, he combined both general and content-specific support (see Figure 3.3). For example, the evidence prompt states: *Provide scientific data to support your claim.* <u>Use the evidence from your table above about the health and changes for the different characteristics of your ecocolumn.</u> The section of the prompt in italics provides general support in that it provides a general definition of evidence. The section of the prompt that is underlined provides content specific support in that it talks about the specific content and investigation that the students just completed. Students need help understanding what the framework is as well as how to construct a scientific explanation for a particular task. These two types of support can be included in one scaffold, like Mr. Cardone's writing prompts, or in multiple scaffolds, such as a visual reminder posted on the wall focused on the general structure and writing prompts for each investigation focused on providing content-specific support.

Fading Curricular Scaffolds. Another characteristic to keep in mind when you design curricular scaffolds for students is the amount of detail in the prompts. When students are first introduced to the framework they require more support and that support should decrease or fade over time (McNeill et al., 2006). Decreasing the amount of detail can be particularly important for the general support since the students eventually internalize the framework and the definitions of the components. At first you want to provide detailed definitions of each component, but as students develop an understanding of these definitions they need less support for the general framework. Table 3.6 illustrates how to fade or decrease support over time. The three examples of prompts provide different levels of support for the general framework. If students have previously received the detailed support prompt,

TABLE 3.6 Fading or Decreasing Support of the Generic Scaffold

Amount of Support	Generic Explanation Scaffold
Detailed Support	**Claim** (Write a statement that responds to the original problem.) **Evidence** (Provide scientific data to support your claim. You should only use appropriate data and include enough data. Appropriate data is relevant for the problem and allows you to figure out your claim. Remember that not all data is appropriate. Enough data refers to providing the pieces of data necessary to convince someone of your claim.) **Reasoning** (In your reasoning statement, connect your claim and evidence to show how your data links to your claim. Also, tell why your data count as evidence to support your claim by using scientific principles. Remember, reasoning is the process where you apply your science knowledge to solve a problem.)
Intermediate Support	**Claim** (Respond to the problem.) **Evidence** (Provide scientific data to support your claim. You should only use appropriate data and include enough data.) **Reasoning** (Connect your claim and evidence. Tell why your data counts as evidence using scientific principles.)
Minimal Support	Remember to include claim, evidence, and reasoning.

when you fade to the minimal support prompt this should serve to activate their knowledge of the definitions of the different components.

Applying the framework to a new content area can be challenging for students even when they are experienced, so they still benefit from the content specific support. They may need help understanding what counts as evidence or reasoning in the new content area. Consequently, the content-specific support, such as that in Table 3.5 or underlined in Mr. Cardone's ecocolumn example, should still be provided to students even when they no longer require reminders of the general framework. This type of support can help them learn how to apply the framework across different science topics.

Check Point

There are many opportunities to incorporate scientific explanations in either writing or discussions in science classrooms. When identifying and designing learning tasks for students, it is important to keep in mind the learning goal of the task and whether the learning task needs to require scientific data and the use of scientific principles to correctly answer the question. After identifying appropriate opportunities for scientific explanations in your science curriculum you can then design the task at a variety of levels of complexity as well as with a range of different scaffolds to support students. In terms of the complexity of the task, it is important to keep in mind the openness of the question, the type of data, the amount of the data, and the inclusion of a rebuttal. After designing the task, incorporating different types of scaffolds such as visual reminders and curricular scaffolds can further be used in order to alter the amount of help provided to students. Providing support for the general framework should decrease or fade over time as students develop a stronger understanding of the framework, while content-specific support is still important when students study new science content to help them understand what counts as appropriate evidence and reasoning in the new topic. Both varying the complexity of the task and designing scaffolds are strategies to support all students in taking part in constructing scientific explanations. Identifying and designing appropriate learning tasks for students is challenging. Once you develop these tasks, there are still other ways to help support students in engaging in scientific explanation. In the next chapter, we will discuss and illustrate other teaching strategies you can use during the lessons in your classroom. Then in future chapters we will shift to focus on assessment to show how scientific explanations can be used as both formative and summative assessments as well as revisit how to support learning over time.

Study Group Questions

1. Examine your current science curriculum for appropriate places to have students construct a scientific explanation. Look for places that include the three key features: (1) Identify Opportunities in the Curriculum, (2) Design Complexity of the Learning Task, and (3) Create Classroom Supports (see Table 3.1).
2. Using the identified places in your curriculum, write specific scientific explanation learning tasks for your students. After creating the learning task, try creating a sample student written response to check the alignment between the learning task and your expectations for your students.
3. What kind of visual representation could you develop that would support your students in constructing scientific explanations? Design the visual representation.
4. What kind of curricular scaffolds could you develop that would support your students in constructing scientific explanations? Design a curricular scaffold.

4

Teaching Strategies to Integrate into Classroom Instruction

How can you provide your students with support as they construct scientific explanations? What types of strategies can you include in your classroom in order to help your students achieve success with this complex practice? Let's consider the following vignette from Ms. Craz's sixth-grade science classroom.

> Ms. Craz's sixth-grade science class is exploring force, motion, and simple machines. As part of the unit, Ms. Craz plans on reinforcing her students' understanding of constructing a scientific explanation and why it is so important in science to do so. In previous lessons, her students learned that a force is either a push or a pull and that a scientific explanation includes a

claim, evidence, and reasoning. In this lesson, she plans on helping her students develop an understanding that using an incline plane with a less steep slope to move an object decreases the amount of force required to move the object.

She begins this new lesson by engaging her students in an investigation in which students lift an object first without an incline plane, then with a very steep incline plane, and finally with a less steep incline plane. In each case, students measure the force required to lift a weighted car 20 centimeters above the ground. Without the incline plane, students lift the car directly off the ground using the spring scale. For the very steep and less steep incline plane, they pull the car up two different lengthened ramps using the spring scale. Ms. Craz thinks this investigation will engage her students and afford an opportunity for students to draw their own relationship about the content from experiencing phenomena, but also provide an opportunity to discuss the purpose of science and the reasons for constructing scientific explanations.

After the class collects their data, Ms. Craz leads a discussion to support her students in making sense of their data. Ms. Craz then asks her students to write a scientific explanation to decide whether or not the slope of the ramp made a difference in terms of how easy or hard it was to move an object. She reminds the students to include a claim, evidence, and reasoning. She uses the think, pair, share structure they used in previous small-group activities. She first has students write down what they thought (think). She then instructs them to discuss their ideas with their partner (pair). She then has the partners share their ideas with two other students (share). Finally, she pulls the class back together and uses ideas from all the groups to develop a class scientific explanation.

The class initially agrees on the claim that the less steep incline plane made it easier to move the object. As evidence, the students state that they needed to apply a greater force to lift the weighted car without an incline plane or with the steep incline plane. However, other students in the class argue that, while it took less force, they had to apply that force for a longer time because to reach the same height they needed to pull the car much further on the less steep incline plane. This idea results in some students questioning the initial claim and what it means for it to be "easier" to move an object. After discussing the alternative explanation, the class agrees that they will define "easier" as requiring less force, which means their initial claim was correct that a less steep inclined plane made it easier. However, the class also agrees that the car had to be moved a further distance with the less steep slope.

Ms. Craz then asks her students, "Why do scientists construct explanations?" She again uses the think, pair, and share structure for students to complete the activity. Before they begin she says, "In writing and discussing

*your response, I want you to think back to why we just wrote a scientific
explanation. What were we trying to do?" After student pairs share their
ideas, she brings the class back together for a discussion. Some groups
say, "To make observations of the world." Other groups respond, "To
learn about the world." Still others state, "To tell you how things worked,"
"to figure things out," and "to agree on what happened as a group using
evidence." Ms. Craz thinks she can make use of the student ideas and lead
them toward the idea that science is about explaining phenomena. Ms. Craz
summarizes the students' comments by stating, "When scientists construct
explanations they do all of these: they make observations, they want to learn
about the world, and they want to know how things work." She then says,
"Another way of stating this is that scientists construct explanations about
things that happen in the world but their explanations need to have sufficient evidence and use reasoning. Science is all about explaining, using
evidence. When scientists construct explanations they are 'learning' about
the world and they use observations and data to provide evidence to support
their ideas."*

This scenario illustrates how a sixth-grade teacher supports her students in
understanding the importance of constructing scientific explanations. Ms. Craz
helps her students to see that writing explanations, based on evidence, is what
scientists do to understand and learn about the world. In so doing, she provides a
rationale for why it is important to write scientific explanations. Our research work
(McNeill & Krajcik, 2008a) shows that providing a rationale is a critical component for students to engage in this scientific practice. In this chapter, we discuss this
strategy and other strategies you can integrate into your classroom that are essential
to supporting students in this practice. We also include video clips of these strategies to illustrate how they can be used in grade 5–8 science classrooms to promote
scientific literacy skills for all students.

Teaching Strategies

In the previous chapter, we focused on how to design learning tasks for scientific
explanation across content and at different levels of complexity. Besides designing the
tasks and developing curricular scaffolds, it is also important for you to provide support
during the science lesson so that all students can take part in this important practice.
The role of the teacher in providing modifications and interventions is essential for
supporting students with learning disabilities, as well as all students, in learning science
(Steele, 2005). Teachers' use of strategies, such as prompting, questioning, coaching,
and modeling, also support English language learners in developing higher levels of
language proficiency, comprehension, and thinking (Echevarria, Vogt, & Short, 2008).

Teaching strategies scaffold your students by providing them with temporary support in order to allow them to achieve a higher level of performance in this complex practice. In our research, we found that using both curricular scaffolds and teaching strategies that aligned with the claim, evidence, and reasoning framework resulted in greater student learning gains for all students in terms of their ability to write scientific explanations (McNeill & Krajcik, 2009). Table 4.1 includes a brief description of eight different teaching strategies. We will describe each of these in more detail as well as discuss video clips of teachers integrating those strategies in their own grade 5–8 science classrooms. The video clips for each strategy are found on the DVD. You may want to watch each clip before reading the description of the teaching strategy.

TABLE 4.1 Eight Different Teaching Strategies for Supporting Students

Teaching strategy	Description
Discuss the Framework	Introduce the framework to students or remind students of the language of claim, evidence, and reasoning after the initial introductory lesson. In addition, you may define or revisit the definitions of the components.
Connect to Everyday Examples	Use examples to illustrate that in everyday life, individuals use evidence and reasoning to decide on answers to questions (e.g., What TV should I buy?) as well as to convince other people (e.g., What is the best movie?).
Provide a Rationale	Describe why a student or a scientist would construct a scientific explanation: (1) science is fundamentally about explaining phenomena, (2) scientists justify as well as convince others of their claims by using evidence and reasoning, and (3) scientists use evidence and reasoning in rebuttals to refute claims by other scientists and other lay people in the community.
Connect to Other Content Areas	Discuss that other content areas, such as social studies, English, and mathematics, can use a similar framework in arguments or persuasive writing.
Model and Critique Examples	Provide examples of both strong and weak scientific explanations using a PowerPoint slide, overhead, or handout. Critique the examples in terms of the strengths and weaknesses.
Provide Students with Feedback	Offer explicit feedback on student writing in either discussion or written feedback, including specific suggestions in terms of the strengths and weaknesses.
Have Students Engage in Peer Critique	Have students trade scientific explanations with partners in class and provide each other with feedback on the strengths and weaknesses.
Debate Student Examples	As a whole class, have students debate the appropriateness and strength of different claims, evidence, and reasoning.

Discuss the Framework

In order for students to be able to construct oral and written scientific explanations, it is important to introduce the framework as well as revisit the framework throughout the school year. Discussing the framework can include introducing the terms claim, evidence, and reasoning, eliciting students' prior ideas about the terms and defining each of the terms. This strategy is essential to supporting the integration of the framework into classroom discussion and writing.

Ms. Nelson Introduces the Framework. In Chapter 2, we discussed video clip 2.1 of Ms. Nelson initially introducing the framework of claim, evidence, and reasoning to her seventh-grade classroom. Ms. Nelson spent approximately 10 minutes discussing the components of claim, evidence, and reasoning as well eliciting her students' ideas about what these terms mean as well as how you justify a claim in science. If you do not recall the clip, you may want to look at it again to observe one way that a teacher introduced the framework to her classroom.

Ms. Moore Introduces the Framework. Video clip 4.1 also shows a teacher introducing the scientific explanation framework to her classroom. In this clip, Ms. Moore introduces the scientific explanation framework of claim, evidence, and reasoning by connecting it to an investigation her students have just completed in which they determined whether fat and soap were the same substance or different substances.[1] She defines each component and then asks her students what that component means as well as what it might look like for the soap and fat example. For instance, after introducing the claim, she calls on a student who says that the claim means "to answer the question" and that her claim was that "fat and soap are different substances." The student quickly understands the concept of claim and provides an appropriate example. After introducing the concept of evidence, Ms. Moore asks her students for examples of evidence. Her students provide a number of appropriate pieces of evidence including different melting points, solubilities, densities, and hardness. After some further probing, her students also state that the

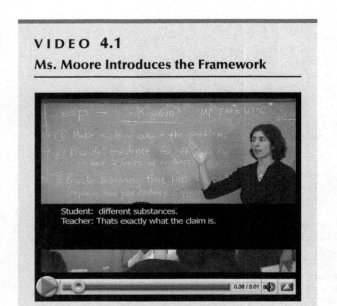

VIDEO 4.1

Ms. Moore Introduces the Framework

Student: different substances.
Teacher: Thats exactly what the claim is.

0.38 / 3.01

---

[1]This is the same science lesson from Brandon's writing in Figure 1.1 in Chapter 1, though Brandon was in Mr. Kaplan's class.

colors were also different, which is another piece of evidence. In the last section of the video, when Ms. Moore asks her students for an example of the reasoning it is interesting that the first student that responds, Zara, repeats the evidence again instead of providing a general scientific principle about different substances having different properties. Ms. Moore probes a little further to push her students to include the more general science principle in their reasoning. She asks her class—"Why are the melting point, density, hardness, color—why are those things important?" A student then provides an appropriate reasoning statement linking the evidence to the claim using a scientific principle in which she states, "Because they are properties, and if substances are alike the properties are alike and the properties weren't alike." Her students needed extra support to move beyond just repeating the evidence to including a general scientific principle. Many teachers find that this reasoning component is challenging for students and can require additional support (McNeill & Krajcik, 2008a), but with this extra support more of her students will be able to take part and further develop their understanding of this important practice and the reasoning component of the framework. This is the first time Ms. Moore introduced the framework to her students. She will continue to use the language of claim, evidence, and reasoning in the future when she asks her students to write scientific explanations either for data they have collected in investigations or data that she provides to them.

Mr. Cardone Revisits the Framework. Since this framework can be new to students, you may want to revisit the components and the definitions of the components in other lessons after the initial introduction of the framework. For example, in video clip 4.2, Mr. Cardone is teaching a lesson to his fifth-grade students about levers and pulleys. He originally introduced the framework of claim, evidence, and reasoning at the beginning of the year, but he revisits the different components with his students before he asks them to write a scientific argument. His students are younger and have had little prior experience supporting claims with evidence and reasoning in either their writing or in discussion. Consequently, he frequently integrates different strategies to support his students. In video clip 4.2, after reviewing the definitions of the three components, he even explicitly says to his students, "Okay, it's all stuff that we've done before and every time we do it you

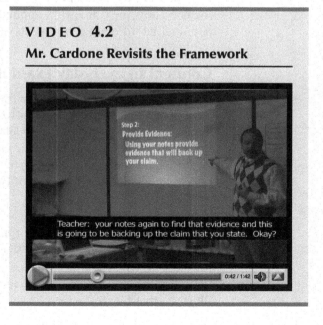

VIDEO 4.2

Mr. Cardone Revisits the Framework

Step 2:
Provide Evidence:
Using your notes provide evidence that will back up your claim.

Teacher: your notes again to find that evidence and this is going to be backing up the claim that you state. Okay?

0:42 / 1:42

guys are getting better and better at it. Now, we have a lot of evidence to use today to formulate a strong claim. So, let's make sure we focus on that." Mr. Cardone acknowledges the previous work the students have done and provides them with positive reinforcement by acknowledging their improvement, because he knows it is a challenging task for his students. In addition to reviewing the different components in a PowerPoint presentation, Mr. Cardone also uses curricular scaffolds on the students' investigation sheets (see for example Figure 3.3) to further provide them with support around the framework.

There are a variety of ways to revisit the framework over time. The video clip of Mr. Cardone illustrates one example of revisiting the language of claim, evidence, and reasoning with his students. Another potential way to revisit the framework would be to ask students if they remember what the different components are as well as the meaning or definition of each component. Sometimes students will use different language to describe a concept than the teacher originally used, which can help support their peers by providing a different description of the concept.

Over time, students will develop a stronger understanding of the framework and the need to explicitly revisit the components and the definitions of each component will become less important. Yet even after the students are familiar with the framework, they may still struggle with how to use the framework in a new content area. For example, if the framework was originally introduced in a lesson on water quality in the next unit about the human body, students may struggle with what does and does not count as appropriate evidence and reasoning. As we discussed in Chapter 3, students may need a combination of supports both for the general framework (e.g., generic explanation scaffolds) as well as how to apply the framework to different content areas (content-specific scaffolds). Consequently, later lessons may include a focus on how the framework applies to a specific content area instead of focusing on defining the different components of the framework.

Connect to Everyday Examples

Using everyday examples can help students draw from their own experiences to develop an understanding of how to justify a claim in science. In everyday situations, people frequently use evidence to answer questions and solve problems; however, what counts as evidence can look quite different. Helping students connect what they are doing in science to these other experiences can help them better understand what is being asked of them when they need to support a claim with evidence and reasoning.

Ms. Nelson Discusses the Best Quarterback. For example, in video clip 2.1 from Chapter 2, Ms. Nelson uses the Who's the best quarterback? example to introduce her students to the claim, evidence, and reasoning framework. She is connecting to a topic that the students already have some knowledge of and experience with to help illustrate that this framework is actually something they use in their own everyday interactions. She uses this everyday example to both introduce and explain the different components.

Mr. Kaplan Discusses the Best Basketball Player. In addition to introducing the scientific explanation framework, connecting the framework to everyday examples can also be used at other points in your instruction to help students develop a more in-depth understanding of why evidence and reasoning are important as well as what counts as evidence and reasoning. For example, in video clip 4.3 Mr. Kaplan is conducting a lesson with his seventh-grade students during the middle of the school year. He had previously introduced the framework, but felt that his students were still struggling with the ideas of evidence and reasoning. Consequently, he decided to use an everyday example: Who is the best basketball player ever? After he introduces the question, two different students offer competing claims. Sierra states that Alan Iverson was the best basketball player ever and Leonard states that Michael Jordan was the best basketball player ever. Video clip 4.3 illustrates the class brainstorming different pieces of evidence to determine the best basketball player ever. The students brainstorm that they could use the following data: (1) average points per game, (2) average free throw percentage, and (3) number of MVP rings. Mr. Kaplan uses this everyday example to illustrate the importance of using evidence to support a claim. If you are debating or want to convince someone of your claim, you want to use multiple pieces of evidence to support that claim.

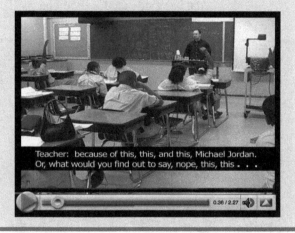

VIDEO 4.3

Mr. Kaplan Discusses the Best Basketball Player

Teacher: because of this, this, and this, Michael Jordan. Or, what would you find out to say, nope, this, this . . .

0.36 / 2.27

Ms. Getty Discusses the Best Band. Ms. Getty also used an everyday example to discuss the framework with her students. Instead of a sports example, she decided to examine the question: Who is the best band? Just as Mr. Kaplan had, she introduced the scientific explanation framework of claim, evidence, and reasoning to her seventh-grade students earlier in the school year. For this lesson, she wrote a model scientific explanation about the Temptations being the best band ever and had her students critique the example as a journal topic before they began a science investigation in which she asked them to write a scientific explanation. Figure 4.1 includes the scientific explanation that she projects for her students as the journal topic.

FIGURE 4.1

Everyday Example—The Temptations

The temptations are the best band ever. They have a popular song and I like it. Therefore, they are the best band ever.

Ms. Getty uses the everyday example to remind her students of the framework and the importance of including explicit evidence and reasoning in their own scientific explanations. Furthermore, students can often use their opinion instead of scientific data as evidence for their claims. This example illustrates that "liking" something is not good evidence, but rather you need to have data. In video clip 4.4, when Ms. Getty asks her students for their critique of the everyday example, the first student immediately brings up the lack of evidence to support the claim that the Temptations are the best band ever. He states, "You've got all your, uh, things covered besides your evidence because you didn't have enough evidence to back it up." When Ms. Getty further probes the student about his thinking, he says that it is not good evidence because "It's your opinion" and states that better evidence would be to "have a vote." Ms. Getty further stresses this idea to her class, that your opinion is not good evidence to support a claim; rather, you need to include data such as numerical data that you could collect from a survey. The class continues to critique the example for not including any reasoning or including enough details. This video clip illustrates a class that has had experience with the claim, evidence, and reasoning framework but continues to need support in order to incorporate this framework into their own writing. The example from Ms. Getty's class also illustrates that using everyday examples can help students distinguish between evidence and opinion—a key aspect of building valid arguments and interpreting arguments presented in the media.

VIDEO 4.4

Ms. Getty Discusses the Best Band

Teacher: So, they are the best band ever. They have a popular song and I like it. So what is it. What's going on?

0:47 / 2:29

Mr. Cardone Discusses the Length of Recess. In his fifth-grade classroom, Mr. Cardone decided to use an everyday example from a language arts writing

FIGURE 4.2

Recess Data to Discuss Claim, Evidence, and Reasoning Framework

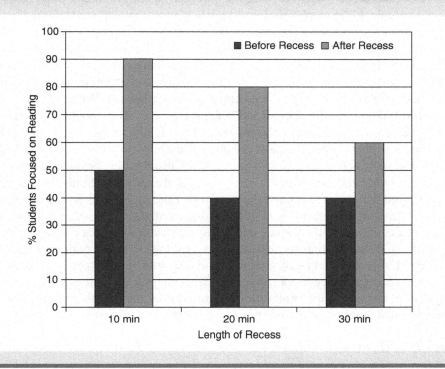

assignment from the previous year to discuss the claim, evidence, and reasoning framework.[2] In fourth grade the students wrote persuasive essays and a number of the students decided to write essays about why their recess should be longer. Consequently, Mr. Cardone found some data from a study about the effect of recess on students' concentration and used that data to discuss the claim, evidence, and reasoning framework. He showed his students the graph in Figure 4.2.

He introduced the graph by telling his students, "Some researchers did a study on recess. They collected data on the percentage of elementary students that were focused on reading before and after recess. They looked at when the recess was ten, twenty, and thirty minutes." He then asked his students, "What argument do you think they made? How long should recess be?" He used this example to illustrate both the importance of using evidence to make claims as well as to introduce the idea of using multiple pieces of evidence to make a claim. The class discussed not

---

[2]Unfortunately, there were technical difficulties with this video clip so it is not included on the DVD. Instead, we just describe what occurred in his classroom.

only what claim they could make from this data (i.e., recess that was 10 minutes long resulted in the greatest increase in focus), but also what other data they might want to collect to better answer the question of how long recess should be (e.g., activities during recess, other outcomes—cognitive skill test, physical health, emotional well-being). Mr. Cardone selected this example, because he knew it was a topic his students cared about and would be passionate about in terms of determining how to answer this question.

These everyday examples provide another avenue to connect what students do in their everyday lives to what we ask them to do in science. Besides sports, music, and recess examples, you can use a wide range of different examples depending on the interests of your students. Other potential questions include: What is the best television show? Who is the best actor? and What is the best school lunch? These different examples all require considering the reasoning behind how to answer the question: What counts as "best"? Is it the most popular? The actor/show that makes the most money? The most nutritious lunch? The examples also require considering what evidence you would need to collect in order to answer the question. In discussing these examples, you may want to discuss the similarities and differences between using the framework in everyday examples as compared to using them in science, such as: How is the evidence different in everyday and scientific examples? What counts as reasoning in the two different contexts? Do everyday examples ever use faulty evidence or reasoning? Using these everyday examples can help students realize they already have knowledge and experiences about how to justify a claim from their everyday lives. Furthermore, discussing the similarities and differences can help them understand how science is a distinct discourse with its own norms in terms of how to justify a claim.

Provide a Rationale

Besides continuing to help students understand what the framework is and how to apply the framework, it is also important to help students understand why they are using the framework. Students can think of science as a static set of facts to memorize. They do not necessarily understand that scientists are constantly trying to make sense of the natural world and use evidence and reasoning to develop and support answers to their questions. Furthermore, students may not realize that scientists can also come up with competing or alternative explanations for the same phenomena and use evidence to determine which is more appropriate. Since students can see science as just the memorization of facts, they can think of the claim, evidence, and reasoning framework as just something else that they have to memorize. You need to help students understand the rationale for why a student or a scientist would construct a scientific explanation that

(1) Science is fundamentally about explaining phenomena;

(2) Scientists justify as well as convince others of their claims by using evidence and reasoning; and

(3) Scientists use evidence and reasoning in rebuttals to refute claims by other scientists and other lay people in the community.

This is a particular method of convincing an individual of a claim, which can differ from other methods individuals may use when they try to convince others of their claim, such as the use of rhetoric, force, or deceptive information. In the scientific community, scientists use evidence to decide between alternative claims, to support a particular claim, and to construct a rebuttal against alternative claims.

In our research we found when teachers both provided their students with the framework and discussed the rationale behind the framework that students had greater learning gains in terms of their ability to write scientific explanations (McNeill & Krajcik, 2008a). Providing students with the rationale does not require a long explanation. Rather, it can be integrated into the way you talk about scientific explanation or integrated into your use of other teaching strategies such as connecting to everyday examples or providing students with feedback.

Mr. Kaplan Discusses the Rationale. For example, in video clip 4.3 in Mr. Kaplan's class discussion of the best basketball player, he uses language such as "how would you prepare to argue or to defend" the claim that you are making? He tries to illustrate to his class that when you are constructing a scientific explanation you should include support in order to convince someone else of your claim through the use of evidence. After discussing the basketball example, Mr. Kaplan has his students write a scientific explanation for whether or not fat and soap are the same substances using properties such as density, melting point, and solubility as evidence. The class then shares some of their written explanations and they discuss them as a class. Video clip 4.5 illustrates how Mr. Kaplan uses similar language when discussing the students' scientific explanations. After two students read their scientific explanations, he stresses again that the students need to be convincing someone of their claim. When a student says that is not what she is trying to do, Mr. Kaplan reinforces the idea by saying, "Well, that is what you—that is what you want to convey.

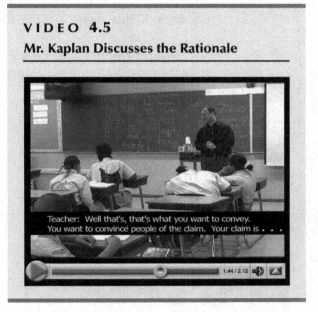

VIDEO 4.5

Mr. Kaplan Discusses the Rationale

Teacher: Well that's, that's what you want to convey. You want to convince people of the claim. Your claim is . . .

1.44 / 2.12

You want to convince people of the claim. Your claim is that these two things are different substances. The evidence that you are using or choosing supports that." In his comments to his class, Mr. Kaplan includes talking about the rationale behind the framework. He emphasizes that the goal of a scientific explanation is to convince, prove, or persuade someone else of the claim that you are making. He tries to help his students understand that the different components are not just a formula or an algorithm that can be mindlessly filled in, but rather the different pieces work together to create a persuasive explanation or argument.

Scientific explanation is a way of knowing, thinking, talking, and writing in science. It is a scientific process to make sense of the world around us. The framework of claim, evidence, and reasoning is a way to break down and make explicit this process for students. Yet it is also important for students to understand the overarching goal so students not only comprehend the individual components, but how they fit together as a whole.

Connect to Other Content Areas

Besides connecting the framework to students' everyday experiences, it can also help students to link the claim, evidence, and reasoning framework to similar practices they engage in during other classes such as social studies, mathematics, and English language arts. For example, students may be asked to write persuasive essays in language arts class, debate historical events in social studies, or prove a theorem in mathematics. Discussing how these different activities are similar to and different from science can support students in seeing how this practice generalizes and is applicable to other fields allowing them to acquire an important twenty-first-century skill that cuts across the different disciplines.

Ms. Nelson Connects to Other Content Areas. For example, video clip 4.6 is later in Ms. Nelson's initial lesson (i.e., video clip 2.1) that introduces the

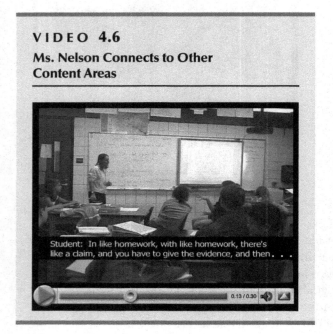

VIDEO 4.6

Ms. Nelson Connects to Other Content Areas

Student: In like homework, with like homework, there's like a claim, and you have to give the evidence, and then. . . .

0.13 / 0.30

scientific explanation framework to her students. In this short clip, one of the students in Ms. Nelson's class spontaneously connects the claim, evidence, and reasoning framework to the work she has to complete for her other classes. The student says, "In like homework—there is like a claim and then you have to give evidence and then you have to do the reasoning. Like in everyday homework." Ms. Nelson then probes the student to find out what subjects she is thinking of in terms of homework. The student responds, "History usually. Math." Ms. Nelson builds on the student's ideas to also talk about how the claim, evidence, and reasoning framework connects to the writing students do in language arts class.

Although in Ms. Nelson's class a student brought up the connection to other content areas, in other cases teachers may need to explicitly bring up the topic of whether the scientific explanation framework is similar or different compared to what students are doing in other classes. Furthermore, it may also help students if their teachers in the different content areas decided to use the same or similar language in order to help students see the commonalities. For example, the teachers in Ms. Nelson's middle school are now working to use the claim, evidence, and reasoning framework across the science, language arts, and history classes. As we mentioned in Chapter 2, a bilingual middle school that we worked with decided to use the framework in math, English language arts, social studies, and science across grades 6–8 to provide their students with common language and experiences across the content areas and the grade levels. This group of teachers decided to alter the language of the framework to be claim, evidence, reasoning, and other explanation (CERO) because they felt that other explanation was more appropriate than rebuttal for math, social studies, and language arts. Furthermore, the majority of their students were native Spanish speakers and cero means "zero" in Spanish. They would remind students that they needed to include CERO in their writing in order to support the claims they were making if they did not want to receive a zero for their work. Helping students make these connections across the content areas can support them in drawing from their previous knowledge and experiences and see the applicability of this framework in different contexts.

Model and Critique Examples

Providing students with examples of scientific explanations as well as critiquing the strengths and weaknesses of those examples can help students understand what it looks like to use the framework across different science content areas. Students can struggle with what counts as an appropriate claim, evidence, or reasoning for different scientific explanation learning or assessment tasks. Discussing examples illustrates what the components look like for different science content areas such as animal behavior, electricity, and the phases of the moon. Furthermore, the teacher can purposefully select or create examples that include common student difficulties when constructing models of scientific explanations in order to provide an avenue to discuss these challenges.

Mr. Cardone Models an Adaptation Example. For example, Mr. Cardone introduced the claim, evidence, and reasoning framework to his fifth-grade science class, which he referred to as a framework for scientific argument in the context of the everyday recess example we discussed earlier in this chapter. In examining his fifth-graders' writing from their first scientific argument, he found that his students had a hard time constructing a claim that specifically answered the question. They

FIGURE 4.3

Claim, Evidence, and Reasoning Adaptation Learning Task

Polar bears live in the Arctic in a cold aquatic environment with ice, snow, and water. They swim and hunt seals in the Arctic Ocean. Polar bears have large front paws that are partially webbed, strong claws on all four paws, and a thick layer of fur.

Write a scientific argument explaining why you think polar bears are able to survive in their natural environment.

also struggled with using data or information as evidence to support the claim. Consequently, he created the scientific argument learning task in Figure 4.3 to specifically talk about some of these student difficulties.

Mr. Cardone begins by showing students a PowerPoint slide with the example in Figure 4.3. Then he tells his class he is going to show them two examples of scientific arguments and that they need to determine which example is stronger and why they think it is stronger. He next projects a slide that includes the two examples in Table 4.2.

Mr. Cardone specifically designed example #2 to not include any of the evidence provided in the learning task. Instead, example #2 focuses on what the polar bears "like" as well as talking more about the characteristics of the Arctic and Hawaii instead of providing evidence for why polar bears are able to survive in particular environments. His hope was that this was a characteristic his students would notice encouraging them to have a conversation about what counts as good evidence.

TABLE 4.2 Models of Strong and Weak Scientific Arguments

Example #1 Polar bears can live in the Arctic, because they have adaptations for the environment. Their webbed paws allow them to swim through the water to catch seals. Their claws also allow them to catch seals. Their fur keeps them warm in the cold environment. Adaptations are characteristics that allow an animal to survive in its environment. Getting food and staying warm are both necessary for an animal to live.

Example #2 Polar bears are able to survive in their natural environment because they like to live where it is cold. They always live somewhere that has lots of snow and ice and water. The Arctic has lots of snow and ice and water, which is why they are able to live there. They would not be able to live someplace that was warm and did not have any snow. For example, they could not live in Hawaii because it is too warm there.

Video clip 4.7 illustrates Mr. Cardone's class discussion of example #2. Since this is the second lesson during the school year that included any mention of claim, evidence, and reasoning, it is not surprising that this language is not included in the fifth-graders' critique of example #2. Yet the students do seem to understand that example #2 is weaker than example #1. The students critique example #2 because it just focuses on what the polar bears like and because it does not have as much detail in it as example #1. Furthermore, they discuss that the reference to Hawaii really does not answer the question of why polar bears can survive in the arctic.

After discussing the strengths and weaknesses of the two examples, Mr. Cardone projects a slide similar to Figure 4.4 in which he clearly identifies the claim, evidence, and reasoning in example #1. In the example he projects, he also changes the color of the font so the claim is yellow, the evidence is orange, and the reasoning is green to further identify the different components. He uses this slide to connect the students' critiques to the language of claim, evidence, and reasoning to support students in understanding that in science, claims are justified through the use of evidence and reasoning. This type of explicit reference can help all students develop an understanding of the framework.

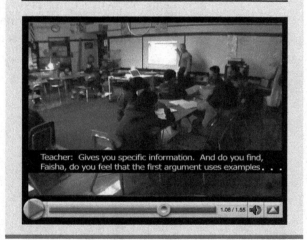

VIDEO 4.7

Mr. Cardone Models an Adaptation Example

Teacher: Gives you specific information. And do you find, Faisha, do you feel that the first argument uses examples . . .

1.08 / 1.55

FIGURE 4.4

Identification of Claim, Evidence, and Reasoning

Argument #1

Polar bears can live in the Arctic, because they have adaptations for the environment (CLAIM). **Their webbed paws allow them to swim through the water to catch seals. Their claws also allow them to catch seals. Their fur keeps them warm in the cold environment (EVIDENCE).** *Adaptations are characteristics that allow an animal to survive in its environment. Getting food and staying warm are both necessary for an animal to live (REASONING).*

Discussing the strengths and weaknesses of these specific examples offered his students a concrete model of what Mr. Cardone's expectations were for their own writing. Mr. Cardone continued to work with his students over the course of the year to understand what counts as evidence and how to include evidence in their own arguments. We will see in a later video clip (i.e., video clip 4.11) that as the year progressed his students became more comfortable in considering how claims are supported with evidence and reasoning.

VIDEO 4.8

Ms. Baker Models a Chemistry Example

Teacher: as notes because it's incorrect data, so don't use that. Um, Michelle what do you think?

1.09 / 1.47

Ms. Baker Models a Chemistry Example. We have worked with a number of seventh-grade science teachers, all of whom used the same middle school chemistry unit, How can I make new stuff from old stuff? (McNeill et al., 2004). One of the lessons in the curriculum asked students to write a scientific explanation about whether or not fat and soap are the same substance or different substances (we showed two examples of Brandon's writing on this in Chapter 1). To help students understand what counted as strong and weak scientific explanations for this learning task, a number of teachers chose to project (either using an overhead or PowerPoint) different examples of scientific explanations. Video clip 4.8 shows Ms. Baker's class critiquing the following example:

Fat is off-white and ivory is milky white. Fat is soft-squishy and soap is hard. Fat is soluble in oil and soap is soluble in water. Fat has a melting point of 47°C and soap has a melting point above 100°C. Fat has a density of 0.92 g/cm³ and soap has a density of 0.84 g/cm³. This is my evidence to show that fat and soap are different substances.

Ms. Baker's seventh-grade students had more experience with the scientific explanation framework as compared to Mr. Cardone's fifth-grade students. Consequently, it is not surprising that the language of claim, evidence, and reasoning is more prevalent in the classroom discussion and in the students' critique of the example. Initially, one of her students critiques the example by saying that it is lacking the claim. Ms. Baker tells her class that in fact the example does have a claim, but it is at the end of the scientific explanation. One aspect that can be confusing for students is if the framework is introduced in the order—claim, evidence and reasoning; students can always expect writing or talk to also occur in this order. It can be difficult for students to understand that it is not the order of the components that is important, but rather that all the components are included and work together to form a cohesive scientific explanation. Another aspect that can be challenging for students is including the reasoning. This example was chosen for critique specifically because it is missing the reasoning. One of the students in Ms. Baker's class correctly identifies the missing component. He states, "It's missing its reasoning." Ms. Baker agrees with the student and reiterates that while it includes all the evidence, it does not include reasoning that articulates why the evidence supports the claim.

Even after students are familiar with the general claim, evidence, and reasoning framework, modeling and critiquing examples as a whole class can help students understand what it looks like to construct a scientific explanation in a specific content area. Examples can also be used to illustrate common student difficulties and to illustrate exemplar scientific explanations so that students understand their teacher's expectations.

Provide Students with Feedback

Another strategy to use with your students is to provide feedback on scientific explanations the students create either in writing or through discussion. This feedback can either occur as part of a whole class discussion in which a student or group of students reads a scientific explanation that they wrote or it can occur as part of individual or group work when you move around the classroom talking to different students. When providing students with feedback on their scientific explanations, it is important to give them specific suggestions both about what aspects are strong as well as what aspects can be improved. If students are just provided with a general statement such as "Good job" or "You need to write more," they will not necessarily know what is good or what is missing from their scientific explanation. Rather, providing specific and descriptive feedback that focuses on both successes and areas that need improvement can have a significant impact on students' science learning (Davies, 2003).

Ms. Hill Provides Students with Feedback. Video clip 4.9 provides an example from Ms. Hill's classrooms. After her students wrote scientific explanations, she asked for a couple of students to stand up and read their writing. In this video clip, Ms. Hill does a nice job providing her student with specific feedback both in terms of what is positive about the example and what needs to be improved. For example, she tells the student, "That is good. I like the way you stated your reasoning," which provides him with specific feedback on what component was good about his explanation. She then asks the class to provide the student with suggestions on how to improve his evidence. After a student offers a suggestion, Ms. Hill summarizes, "You need to elaborate on whatever data, whatever evidence you cite. Don't just say they are different colors— what colors are they?" Ms. Hill's expectation was that her students' evidence would include specific observations or measurements from their investigations. She clearly articulated that expectation to her students in the feedback she provided as part of a whole-class discussion.

VIDEO 4.9

Ms. Hill Provides Students with Feedback

Teacher: Okay, so when you rewrte it, and, have you put it in your book? You may want to make a comment . . .

1.06 / 1.55

Feedback can take a variety of forms including both comments and questions as well as focus on either the structure of the scientific explanation or the understanding of the science content. Feedback can include specific comments on a scientific explanation that a student has written or spoken, such as the suggestions provided above by Ms. Hill about the student's reasoning and evidence. Her comments focused on the claim, evidence, and reasoning structure. Another form that can be useful is to use questions that target the different components of the framework. Table 4.3 provides some examples of potential questions.

These questions could be used during a full-class discussion to encourage students to support their claims as well as when students are working individually or in groups. For example, you may be moving around the classroom and reading students' work as they are writing. You may find that one student has not included any reasoning in her scientific explanation; consequently you may ask her a question such as: Why does your evidence support your claim? As students become more comfortable and confident with the scientific explanation framework, these types of questions may become less prevalent in the classroom because they no longer need the added support.

TABLE 4.3 Examples of Questions to Use to Provide Students with Feedback

Component	Example Questions
Claim	• What is your claim for the question? • What claim can you make based on your data?
Evidence	• What is your evidence for that claim? • Do you have enough evidence to support that claim? • Is there other evidence that would support that claim? • Is there evidence that would suggest another claim would be more appropriate? • What do you think of the quality of the evidence for the claim?
Reasoning	• What is your reasoning? • Why does that evidence support the claim? • What scientific principles or concepts did you use to make sense of your data?

Feedback can also focus on the students' understanding of the science content demonstrated in their scientific explanation. For example, if the student in Ms. Hill's class included an inappropriate piece of evidence, such as mass, illustrating that he was confused about what did and did not count as a property, Ms. Hill could have focused her comments on helping the student understand that science principle. For example, she could have stated, "I noticed you used mass as one piece of evidence that they were different substances. I want you to think about that idea. Does having a different mass provide evidence that two objects are different substances? For example, here is a small and large piece of chalk [holds up two pieces]. Would these have the same mass? Are they different substances?" Providing specific and detailed feedback can help students develop a stronger understanding both of scientific explanations and of the science content. In Chapter 6, we will provide additional examples of teacher feedback for students when we discuss using rubrics to assess student learning and inform instruction. Providing feedback takes time; however, substantial evidence exists that providing feedback is one of the most effective ways to support all students in learning challenging ideas and practices (Pellegrino, Chudowsky, & Glaser, 2001).

Have Students Engage in Peer Critique

Besides providing feedback to students on their scientific explanations, students can provide feedback to each other. This can occur in a format similar to the video clip 4.9 from Ms. Hill's classroom where one student reads his or her explanation and the whole class provides the student with feedback. Another way to structure this strategy is to have students work in pairs or in small groups where students trade their written scientific explanations and then each individual in the class receives feedback. Providing constructive feedback to their peers can be a challenging task for students. Consequently, it can be helpful to provide students with suggestions or a structure to guide them in the feedback they provide their peers.

Ms. Nelson Engages Her Students in Peer Critique. To help her students provide each other with useful feedback, Ms. Nelson had her students identify and provide feedback on the three components of the scientific explanation framework—claim, evidence, and reasoning. Specifically, she had each student trade papers with another member of the class. She told them to circle the claim, number the pieces of evidence, and underline the reasoning for their peer's paper. Students then used this identification process to provide their partner with specific suggestions on how to improve their scientific explanation. Figure 4.5 is an example of one of the student's scientific explanations from the peer review process.

Within the figure example, the scientific explanation did not include any pieces of evidence, which was the major critique provided by the student's peer. Although the student clearly states a claim and provides some reasoning in the discussion of properties, the student does not include any of the scientific data collected during the investigation to support his claim.

Video clip 4.10 begins with Ms. Nelson providing these directions to her students. The clip then focuses on two pairs of students in Ms. Nelson's class providing each other with feedback and discussing the feedback. The pair on the left initially discuss Josh's scientific explanation, which his partner says only has a claim. Josh responds by saying, "I thought I had some facts." His partner reads Josh's scientific explanation stating, "All you say is that soap and fat are different because they have different attributes and properties. But you don't say anything else." Josh

FIGURE 4.5
Peer Review of Scientific Explanation

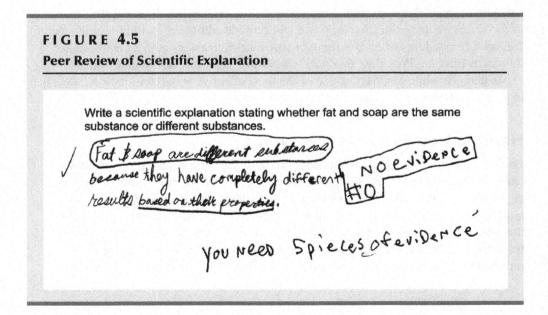

agrees that he is lacking support. This conversation between the two boys on the left illustrates that they are able to provide critical and specific feedback to each other. The camera then focuses on the pair on the right and their discussion of one student's scientific explanation. Initially, the two disagree on how many pieces of evidence are included in the scientific explanation, but through discussion they are able to finally agree that he has included five pieces of evidence to support his claim. This conversation illustrates that when provided with a specific structure for peer review students are able to successfully engage in peer critique around their scientific explanations.

VIDEO 4.10

Ms. Nelson Engages Her Students in Peer Critique

Teacher: reasoning. Could you underline reasoning. Okay, so you're going to do three things. What I want . . .

1.23 / 3.14

Having students provide each other with feedback can allow every student in the class to receive constructive suggestions on how to improve their scientific explanations. Furthermore, the act of critiquing can expose students to other examples of scientific explanations as well as to thinking critically about what it means to construct a strong explanation. Discussions around the critique can further help students understand what the different components should look like in their own science writing.

Debate Student Examples

The last strategy focuses on a full-class debate. Students construct a scientific explanation and then as a class debate the appropriateness and strength of the different components—claim, evidence, and reasoning. In this debate, students share their different scientific explanations and provide each other with feedback, and the teacher in turn provides the students with feedback. The goal is to as a class decide on the strongest claim, evidence, and reasoning. The strategy offers a different activity structure that combines some of the characteristics of the previous three strategies (to model and critique examples, provide students with feedback, and have students engage in peer critique).

Mr. Cardone Leads His Class in a Debate. During the construction piece of this strategy, students write a scientific explanation with various degrees of support. In Mr. Cardone's class, he decided his fifth-grade students needed more support and models of what counted as appropriate claim, evidence, and reasoning. Although the majority of his students were able to provide claims by this point during the school year, many of the fifth-grade students still struggled with justifying those claims with appropriate evidence and reasoning. Consequently, he provided his students with the activity sheet in Figure 4.6 that focused on an argument which

FIGURE 4.6

Claim, Evidence, and Reasoning Student Sheet

Directions

The 4th graders have just finished a number of experiments testing how different variables affect the speed of a car. Mr. Cardone asks them to write an argument that answers the following question: How can you design a car to go the fastest? Circle the choices below that you think would create the strongest argument.

CLAIM

Circle ONE of the following.

  A. My car will go the fastest, because I will make it really strong.

  B. The car with the lightest load being pulled by the largest force will go the fastest.

  C. How fast a car goes is determined by how far it travels in a certain time.

EVIDENCE

Circle TWO of the following.

  A. The car with only one block on the car took 1 second to travel across the table while the car with three blocks took 3 seconds.

  B. We always built our cars carefully and they traveled really fast.

  C. Car companies, like Ford, try to build light cars because they will travel faster.

  D. The car that was pulled by 5 washers took 2 seconds to travel across the table while the car with 1 washer took 7 seconds.

  E. Our group had a lot of fun building and testing our cars, except for the one day that our car kept breaking.

  F. Our experiments showed that light cars travel faster.

REASONING

Circle ONE of the following.

  A. The data from our experiments shows us how to build our car. Since the data shows that fast cars have a light load and fast cars are pulled by a large force then this is how we should build our car.

  B. Since car companies and race cars have cars that are really light and have large engines this means we should design our car in the same way. It should have a light load and be pulled by a large force.

  C. The speed was determined by how many seconds it took for the car to travel across the table. The car with less blocks had a lighter load and it traveled faster. The car that was pulled by more washers was pulled by a greater force and it traveled faster.

answered the question: How can you design a car to go the fastest? This learning task aligned with a previous science learning goal where the students conducted multiple investigations exploring how changing the force on a car affected the speed of the car (i.e., greater force resulted in a faster car) and how changing the mass of a car affected the speed of the car (i.e., greater mass resulted in a slower car). Instead of having the students write their own claim, evidence, and reasoning, Mr. Cardone provided his students with examples that represented some aspects of the framework that were challenging for his students.

If you look at Figure 4.6, the two strongest pieces of evidence are Evidence A and Evidence D. Both these pieces of evidence provide specific data from an investigation that supports Claim B that "the car with the lightest load being pulled by the largest force will go the fastest." Evidence B and F were included on the student sheet because Mr. Cardone's students often included in their evidence links to their investigations, but in very general terms instead of detailed data. He wanted to stress that they should use specific observations and measurements as evidence, instead of just describing the experiment in general. Evidence C was included to help students consider that the strongest evidence should come from specific data and not just prior everyday knowledge they had about the world. Evidence E was included because sometimes his students focused on what they enjoyed or what they liked instead of specific data from an investigation.

Video clip 4.11 focuses on the debate about the evidence component of the scientific argument. The clip is approximately 10 minutes long and includes excerpts from Mr. Cardone introducing the task to his students, the students working in groups to select the two strongest pieces of evidence, the students' presentation of that evidence to the class, and the class debate to decide which two pieces of evidence are the strongest. The actual class time for these activities was approximately 35 minutes, but we edited the clip to provide examples of the different activities during the class. The clip begins with Mr. Cardone explaining to the class that they need to work with their group to select the two best pieces of evidence to support the claim. As the students work in groups, Mr. Cardone moves around the classroom and asks different groups questions to encourage them to reflect on why their evidence supports their claim. The group he talks to in the video has selected evidence D and evidence F as their two pieces of evidence. He encourages the group to really think about what the claim is stating and consider whether the evidence

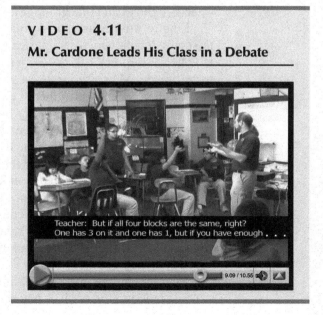

VIDEO 4.11

Mr. Cardone Leads His Class in a Debate

Teacher: But if all four blocks are the same, right? One has 3 on it and one has 1, but if you have enough . . .

9.09 / 10.55

supports that claim. He starts by talking to the group about evidence D, which is one of the two strongest pieces of evidence. He asks the students questions to help them connect evidence D to the part of the claim that focuses on force. He then asks them to think about evidence F connecting to the claim. Mr. Cardone does not provide the students with the right answer (i.e., that evidence F is too general), but rather asks probing questions to encourage the students to discuss and think through their choices.

Next, Mr. Cardone has each group present which two pieces of evidence they selected and why they selected those two pieces of evidence to the entire class. When introducing this activity, he tells the class, "Remember, if they do not have the same reasoning or the same evidence, you are going to have to think about why their evidence either does not make sense or maybe they are going to be able to convince you that yours was not making as much sense." He encourages the students to listen to each other with an open mind so that as a class they can determine the two best pieces of evidence. The first group he calls on to present selected evidence D and evidence F. In presenting evidence F, their rationale for their choice was just to repeat the evidence again, while for evidence D their rationale includes describing how it links to the claim. After they present, one student, Selenes, asks a question about whether the evidence or reasoning comes from your own personal experience. Mr. Cardone states that they will discuss this more later. After the first group presents, Mr. Cardone calls on the other five groups and the video jumps to the presentation of the last student group, which includes Selenes. Her group selected evidence B and F. In discussing their rationale for their choice, they link it back to the original question instead of explicitly linking the evidence to the claim. For the six student groups, two groups select D and F, two groups select A and D, one group selects A and F, and one group selects B and F.

Finally, after hearing everyone's rationale for their choices, Mr. Cardone has the class debate which two pieces are the strongest. The class begins by discussing whether or not they believe evidence A is good evidence. After Dashawn presents his rationale, Mr. Cardone stresses the importance of using "real numbers" as evidence. Then Selenes says that "I changed my mind and I agree with those tables." This suggests that she was really listening to the choices made by her peers and their explanations for why they had selected evidence A. Selenes is developing a stronger understanding that the evidence should come from the data collected in investigations in class, rather than from personal experience. After the class agrees on evidence A, one student states that the other piece of evidence should be evidence D. Mr. Cardone continues to use probing questions to support the students to listen to each other, consider the strength of each piece of evidence, and think through the rationale behind their choices. After some discussion, the class decides that evidence A and evidence D are the strongest pieces of evidence to support their claim.

By debating the different claims, evidence, and reasoning as a class, the students listened to the choices and rationales provided by their peers. This offered them multiple models of different arguments and feedback on the strengths and weaknesses of those arguments. Because of the complex nature of this strategy, we would not suggest using it to initially introduce the claim, evidence, and reasoning framework. For example, in Mr. Cardone's case this discussion happened with his fifth-graders in March when they had originally been introduced to the framework at the beginning of the school year. Yet the strategy can be a beneficial way to engage students in discussing and reflecting on how to support a claim in science.

Supporting All Learners

As we previously mentioned, the strategies discussed throughout this chapter can help support all learners, including English language learners and students with special needs, to better succeed in science. Using a variety of different strategies in your classroom can provide students with multiple means to become engaged in and learn science, which aligns with the recommendations from the Universal Design for Learning (UDL) framework. UDL makes learning accessible for all students including students with sensory disabilities, learning disabilities and language or cultural differences (Rose & Meyer, 2002). The UDL framework calls for: (1) multiple means of engagement, (2) multiple means of representation, and (3) multiple means of expression. The scientific explanation framework of claim, evidence, and reasoning as well as the different instructional supports (e.g., Chapter 3) and teaching strategies (e.g., Chapter 4) that we have discussed align with the UDL recommendations.

In terms of multiple means of engagement, using the various teaching strategies provides different opportunities to engage and interest students in the science. Students differ in terms of what interests them and motivates them. For example, some students may be engaged by connecting the scientific explanation framework to everyday examples, such as Mr. Kaplan with basketball and Ms. Getty with music and Mr. Cardone with recess. These connections may interest students because they see how they can use what they already know from their everyday experiences. Other students may be more engaged by doing peer critique, because they enjoy working one on one with their peers and helping each other with their learning, while other students may be more engaged by the full-class debate in Mr. Cardone's class, because they enjoy using evidence to convince others of the claim and debating alternative explanations. Incorporating different strategies in your classroom increases the opportunity to engage multiple types of learners in this complex scientific inquiry practice, which may not occur in a classroom that only focuses on one strategy.

Multiple means of representation stresses the importance of providing learners with different ways of acquiring knowledge through visual and auditory means. Since no one means of representing the content will be ideal for all students, it is important to include different methods in your own teaching. In Chapter 3, we discussed a variety of different ways to represent and support students in being able to construct scientific explanations such as using visual representations and curricular scaffolds, both of which provide a visual representation of the framework. A number of the strategies in this chapter provide different auditory means to support student learning such as teacher modeling, teacher feedback, student feedback, and whole-class debates. These different strategies can also be supported by visual means, such as the reminders Ms. Nelson wrote on the board as part of the peer critique to circle the claim, number the evidence, and underline the reasoning. Using these different types of support provides students with multiple representations to better enable all students to successfully construct scientific explanations.

Finally, multiple means of expression includes the importance of providing learners with multiple ways to demonstrate what they know. Although we often focus on student writing in this book, students can also demonstrate their understanding through discussions, presentations, or graphic forms. For example, students could construct posters where they provide a claim and support it with evidence and reasoning using photographs from their experiment and other visual representations of the different components of the framework. Students can also construct their scientific explanations orally such as in a debate, or if you want to provide individual students the opportunity to orally construct their scientific explanations you could ask them to audio record their explanations. Furthermore, the amount of the support for student writing can be varied from students circling the appropriate claim, evidence, and reasoning (Figure 4.6), to providing students with curricular scaffolds (Figure 3.3), to providing students with an open-ended writing task. Incorporating a variety of techniques and strategies in your classroom will support all your students in being able to successfully engage in this important scientific practice.

Check Point

In this chapter, we discussed and illustrated eight different teaching strategies that you can use during your class to support all students in scientific explanation: (1) discuss the framework, (2) connect to everyday examples, (3) provide a rationale, (4) connect to other content areas, (5) model and critique examples, (6) provide students with feedback, (7) have students engage in peer critique, and (8) debate student examples. These strategies can help support students in constructing scientific explanations in both writing and talk in which they appropriately justify their claims with evidence and reasoning. We are not suggesting that all these strategies be integrated in every lesson, but rather they are a toolbox of resources that you can draw from when you feel your students are struggling with various aspects of this complex task. Furthermore, these teaching strategies need to align with the other supports you include in your classroom, such as visual reminders and scaffolds on student investigation sheets. Using both curricular scaffolds and teaching strategies aligned with the framework will result in greater student learning gains (McNeill & Krajcik, 2009). By supporting students in a variety of ways you are more likely to meet the needs of all your learners since different strategies will be more effective for different individuals. Building these strategies into your classroom will enhance not only the quality of writing, but also the quality of the conversations your students have. In the next two chapters, we shift our focus to talk about assessments; we will describe how to develop scientific explanation assessment tasks that can be used as both formative and summative assessments as well as how to create and use rubrics to assess students' strengths and weaknesses. Finally, in the last chapter, we focus on developing a classroom culture around scientific explanation and other strategies that will support your students learning over time.

Study Group Questions

1. Of the eight strategies presented, which strategy could you incorporate into your classroom mostly easily? Why? How will you use that strategy?
2. Of the eight strategies presented, which strategy would be most challenging to use in your classroom? Why?
3. What everyday examples would you use to help your students understand the structure of scientific explanations? Write a sample scientific explanation for the everyday example, considering what would count as appropriate evidence and reasoning.
4. Design a scientific explanation question for science content that your students are familiar with. Use that question and create some examples of strong and weak scientific explanations. How would you use these examples with your students?

Developing Assessment Tasks and Rubrics

How can you design assessment tasks that allow you to assess your students' abilities to construct scientific explanations? How can you create assessment tasks that also align with the key science content learning goals that you need to address? Let's consider the following vignette that shows how a sixth-grade teacher goes about his development of an assessment task.

Mr. McRobbie, a sixth-grade science teacher, is teaching a unit on rocks and minerals. He wants to create a scientific explanation assessment task that aligns with his state standards and will allow him to assess whether his students understand the key science concepts in the unit. He selects the following content standard:

Rock Formation—Rocks and rock formations bear evidence of the minerals, materials, temperature/pressure conditions, and forces that created them (from the State of Michigan standards).

He also selects the following inquiry standard:

> *Use multiple sources of information to evaluate strengths and weaknesses of claims, arguments, or data (from the State of Michigan standards).*

In creating the assessment item, Mr. McRobbie carefully considers both the content standard about rocks and minerals and the inquiry standard about constructing scientific explanations, because he wants the assessment item to assess students' understandings of both ideas. Consequently, he designs an assessment item that will require his students to analyze data, apply their understandings of minerals, and to write a scientific explanation. Here is his assessment item:

> *Ben has an unknown mineral and he is trying to figure out the identity of the mineral. The unknown mineral is white, when he rubs it across a streak plate it leaves a white line, it is shiny, and when he breaks it the pieces are smooth and it always breaks in the same pattern. He also tested the hardness and it is around a 6 or a 7.*
>
> *Based on the color, Ben decided that the unknown is talc, feldspar, or quartz. He decided to look up other information about these three minerals. He placed the information he found in a table.*

Mineral	Color	Streak	Hardness	Luster	Other
Talc	White	White	1	Pearly	Greasy feel
Feldspar	White, Red, Green	White	6	Glassy	Cleavage
Quartz	White, other colors	None	7	Glassy	No cleavage, curved fracture

> *Using the information in the table, and data Ben collected on the unknown, write a scientific explanation stating what you think is the identity of the unknown mineral. Justify not only your choice, but also why you did not select the other two minerals.*

After designing the assessment item, Mr. McRobbie writes a potential ideal student response to help him think about how he would like his students to respond. He hopes his students will construct a claim that the unknown mineral is feldspar and use evidence from Ben's investigation and the table to support the claim. For example, the students could include as evidence that the unknown mineral has a white streak and a hardness of 6 or 7 and feldspar has a white streak and a hardness of 6. In the students' reasoning, he wants them to explain that properties help you identify minerals and the rebuttal should include evidence or reasoning for why the unknown mineral is not talc or quartz. For example, the students could include in their rebuttal that talc has a hardness of 1 and quartz does not have a streak, which are both different compared to the unknown mineral.

Finally, based on a workshop he attended at the state science conference, Mr. McRobbie reviews the quality of the assessment item, considering three criteria: (1) whether the knowledge in the standards is needed to correctly answer the item, (2) whether the item requires any additional content knowledge not in the standard, and (3) whether the item will be comprehensible to all his students.[1] He realizes that the assessment item made a match with only a portion of the content standard. Students will need to understand what minerals are and how to identify minerals to answer the question, but the item does not match well with the rock formation aspects of the standard. He reasons that assessment items often do not match an entire standard so he feels okay about only addressing part of a standard. Mr. McRobbie also realizes that students will need additional content knowledge that you can use properties to identify substances, which is not explicitly stated in the standard. However, based on their work in the previous chemistry unit and the current rocks and minerals unit, he feels that students will have an understanding of this idea. Finally, he feels that the context of the item will be comprehensible to all his students because the students completed similar investigations during the rocks and minerals unit.

Overall, Mr. McRobbie is pretty satisfied with the quality of the item based on his review. He feels that the item will allow him to assess if his students can apply both their understanding of minerals and their understanding of how to construct a scientific explanation. He is interested to see how his students will respond to the item.

This vignette illustrates how a teacher can design an assessment item that combines students' understanding of a science concept and their ability to construct a scientific explanation. Through the careful design and review of assessment items, assessments can be created to better match and assess content and inquiry standards. Although the process does require time, it ensures that you design assessment tasks that promote learning and engage students in the construction of scientific explanations. In this chapter, we describe the six steps we use to design both formative and summative assessment items and the associated rubrics. We will take you through several examples that use this process so that we can illustrate what the steps look

---

[1]As we will discuss later in the chapter, the necessity, sufficiency and comprehensibility criteria is based on the work of George DeBoer from Project 2061.

like in practice in order to create assessment items that align with the learning goals of both the science content and scientific explanation.

Overview of the Development Process

Creating assessment tasks that will allow you to assess both students' understanding of scientific explanations and key science concepts is a challenge, yet critical to support all your students in developing understanding. The development process we describe will allow you to explicitly align assessment tasks with the scientific explanation framework and key science concepts to allow you to assess these learning goals (McNeill & Krajcik, 2008b). The goal is not for students to be able to construct scientific explanations in the absence of content, but rather to support students in using their understanding of the science concepts to make sense of data and justify their claims with appropriate evidence and reasoning. In this way, all your students will develop core ideas and twenty-first-century skills. This assessment process can be used to develop both formative assessments that are used to improve teaching and learning as well as summative assessments that are cumulative assessments to evaluate the quality of student work against some standards (NRC, 2001). In the next chapter, we discuss how assessments can be used in both capacities using examples of student work. This chapter focuses on describing our development process, which consists of six steps that are summarized in Table 5.1.

We will describe each step in more detail using two cases to illustrate the process. The first case focuses on Mr. Cardone's fifth-grade science classes. At the end of the school year, he gave his students a test to assess the content and scientific inquiry practices they developed over that year, one of the key science concepts being food webs. Consequently, we worked with Mr. Cardone using our development

TABLE 5.1 Development Process for Scientific Explanation Assessment Tasks
Step 1: Identify and unpack the content standards
Step 2: Select scientific explanation level of complexity
Step 3: Create learning performance
Step 4: Write the assessment task
Step 5: Review the assessment task
Step 6: Develop specific rubric

process for assessment tasks to design a writing assessment item about food webs in which his students had to support their claims with appropriate evidence and reasoning. The second case study focuses on an assessment item we wrote for an end of unit test for a seventh-grade chemistry curriculum. A number of seventh-grade teachers used the test after teaching the 8-week chemistry unit, *How can I make new stuff from old stuff?* (McNeill et al., 2004). The specific assessment item we focus on in this chapter asks students to write a scientific explanation about whether or not a chemical reaction occurred. For each of the six steps of the development process, we will first describe the process in general and then use the two cases to illustrate what the step looks like in practice. Following this process will support you in developing assessment items that align with key learning goals that support all your students in learning core ideas.

Step 1: Identify and Unpack the Content Standard

The first step in the process is to identify and unpack the content standard. In terms of identifying standards, it is important to select national or state standards that target the key science concepts you address in your classroom. Examining the standards and selecting the appropriate ones can also help you determine what concepts are key aspects of the standards and essential for science literacy. After we select a standard, we then go through a process of "unpacking." Unpacking has two components. First, one standard can often contain many different science ideas. In order to develop an in-depth understanding of the standard, it helps to break it down into related science ideas and to clarify each science idea in terms of its meaning and relationship to the other ideas in the standard. Second, it also helps to consider common student misconceptions, alternative conceptions or non-normative ideas for that science concept. Students often come to science class with many ideas about the natural world from their previous experiences either in their everyday lives or in school, which do not align with current scientific theories (Driver, Guesne, & Tiberghien, 1985). Students weakly hold some of these ideas so they can easily develop more appropriate scientific understandings, while other ideas are more deeply held in part because they are connected to students' previous experiences. More deeply held ideas take time and multiple experiences in order for students to develop understandings that align with established science ideas. Explicitly incorporating student alternative conceptions into the assessment item can allow you to assess whether or not the students in your classroom hold alternative conceptions about a particular science concept. Furthermore, knowing student alternative conceptions will help you in planning your instruction so that you can support all your students. This unpacking process can help clarify what science ideas to target in the item as well as common student difficulties to incorporate into the item. We will illustrate this unpacking process for the two different cases.

Fifth-grade Food Web Case—Unpacking

As we mentioned previously, one of the key science content learning goals in Mr. Cardone's fifth-grade science classroom was food webs. The NRC national standards (1996) include a key science learning goal for grades 5–8 focused on food webs, which is listed in Table 5.2 along with the clarification of the standard and potential student alternative conceptions. The standard includes the different types of organisms in a food web, their function in the food web, and the relationships between the organisms. The clarification elaborates on these different organisms by defining producers, consumers, and decomposers in terms of how they obtain energy and nutrients. The clarification also elaborates on how energy flows through a food web. The complex relationships in a food web mean that organisms are influenced not only by the organisms that they directly eat or eat them, but also by indirect relationships with organisms that are two or more steps removed. For example, in an aquatic food web a fish, such as a tuna, is impacted not only by the shrimp it eats, but also by the phytoplankton the shrimp eat. If the population size of the phytoplankton decreased, there would be a decrease in population size of both the shrimp and the tuna.

Research examining students' understandings of food webs has found that late elementary and early middle school students often have a number of alternative conceptions (AAAS, 1993; AAAS, 2009; Gallegos, Jerezano, & Flores, 1994). Table 5.2 lists some of those student difficulties. One alternative conception of grade 5–8 students is in understanding the relationships between organisms in a food web that are not directly linked to each other. Students may incorrectly think that only organisms directly connected to each other impact the population size of that organism. For example, in the aquatic food web described previously, students may think that if the phytoplankton population decreased that it would have no impact on the tuna population, because the phytoplankton are not directly linked to the tuna. When designing assessment tasks, it is important to keep student alternative conceptions in mind in order to embed them in the task to determine whether or not the students are struggling with that science idea. We will return to this alternative conception about indirect relationships in food webs in the design of the assessment task.

Seventh-grade Chemical Reaction Case—Unpacking

The seventh-grade case focuses on an end-of-unit test developed for an 8-week chemistry curriculum that included chemical reactions as one of the key content learning goals. Table 5.3 includes the standard focusing on chemical reactions from AAAS, the clarification of that standard and potential student alternative conceptions.

TABLE 5.2 Unpacking of Food Web Standard

Standard	Clarifying the Standard	Student Alternative Conceptions
"Populations of organisms can be categorized by the function they serve in an ecosystem. Plants and some micro-organisms are producers—they make their own food. All animals, including humans, are consumers, which obtain food by eating other organisms. Decomposers, primarily bacteria and fungi, are consumers that use waste materials and dead organisms for food. Food webs identify the relationships among producers, consumers, and decomposers in an ecosystem." (NRC, 1996, C: 4/2, 5–8)	An ecosystem consists of both living organisms and nonliving factors that function together in an area to produce a sustainable unit. Ecosystems can be as large as a forest and as small as a rotting log. Living organisms in an ecosystem can have different functions in terms of how they obtain energy and nutrients. Producers are organisms that make their own food, such as plants and some microorganisms. Consumers are organisms that obtain their food by eating, such as animals (including humans). Decomposers are organisms that eat waste materials from other organisms and dead organisms as food. Bacteria and fungi are both examples of decomposers. A food web is a representation that shows the feeding relationships between organisms in an ecosystem, including how energy and nutrients are transferred from one organism to another. Organisms in a food web (such as producers, consumers, and decomposers) are directly impacted by the organisms that they either eat or that eat them. Organisms are also indirectly impacted by organisms two or more steps away in the food web, because of the energy flow through the food web. The complex relationships in a food web often mean that if the population size of one organism changes it has an impact on multiple other organisms in the food web.	• Students believe that there is no relationship between the size of the predator and prey populations. For example, if the prey population is small, students do not think the predator population has to be small. • Students think that food webs include consumers, but not producers. • Students think that if the population size of one organism in a food web changes, it will only impact other organisms that are directly linked to that organism. For example, they think if an organism eats or is eaten by another organism it will be impacted. They have difficulty understanding the relationships or impacts of organisms that are two or more steps away.

101

Step 1:
Identify and
Unpack the
Content
Standard

TABLE 5.3 Unpacking the Chemical Reaction Standard

Standard	Clarifying the Standard	Student Alternative Conceptions
Substances react chemically in characteristic ways with other substances to form new substances with different characteristic properties. (AAAS, 2009, 4D/M11**)	Substances are made of one material throughout and have distinct properties, such as melting point, density, and solubility. A chemical reaction is a process where new substances are made from old substances. One type of chemical reaction is when two substances are mixed together and they interact to form new substance(s). The properties of the new substance(s) are different from the old substance(s). When scientists talk about "old" substances that interact in the chemical reaction, they call them reactants. When scientists talk about new substances that are produced by the chemical reaction, they call them products.	• Students think other processes, such as freezing, boiling, and mixtures, are chemical reactions. • Students do not understand the relationship between the new substance and the old substance—that the new substance is created from the old substance. Instead, they can think that the old substance disappeared and the new substance appeared. • Students can have difficulty understanding what characteristics count as properties that can be used to differentiate between substances. For example, they can incorrectly use the size or volume of an object to identify a substance.

A major component of this standard is the idea that a chemical reaction produces new substances from old substances. In order to fully understand this concept, students also need to know that a substance is made of the same material throughout and that the way you identify a substance is through the use of distinct properties, such as melting point, density, and solubility, which are independent of the amount of the sample. Consequently, in order to determine whether a chemical reaction has occurred after combining substances, you need to identify and compare properties before and after mixing. Students have a variety of alternative conceptions about chemical reactions (AAAS, 1993; AAAS, 2009; Eilks, Moellering, & Valanides, 2007). For example, one issue students struggle with is what to count as evidence that a chemical reaction occurred; they struggle with what characteristics of substances are properties that can be used to identify substances (e.g., melting point and density) compared to what characteristics cannot be used to identify a substance (e.g., mass or volume). Consequently, when designing the chemical reaction scientific explanation assessment item, we purposefully included some data that was not appropriate to use to determine if a chemical reaction had occurred (e.g., volume). We wanted to determine whether or not students held this potential alternative conception.

Step 2: Select Scientific Explanation Level of Complexity

The next step in designing the assessment item is to select the scientific explanation level of complexity. Specifically, you want to consider the level of the complexity of the framework as well as potential difficulties your students have with constructing scientific explanations. Do you want students to only provide three components (e.g., claim, evidence, and reasoning) or to also include the fourth component of the rebuttal? For each of the components, what level of complexity do you want students to include in their responses? In Chapter 2, Table 2.3 included detailed descriptions of four different variations of the scientific explanation framework with varying degrees of complexity determined by the number of components and the characteristics of each component. Table 5.4 summarizes those four different variations. The first variation includes the three components with relatively simple definitions of each component. Variations two and three still just consist of claim, evidence, and reasoning, but the complexity in both the evidence and reasoning

TABLE 5.4 Summary of Four Different Variations of the Scientific Explanation Framework

Variation	Description of Framework
Variation #1	1. Claim 2. Evidence 3. Reasoning

Variation #2	1. Claim
	2. Evidence
	  • Appropriate
	  • Sufficient
	3. Reasoning

Variation #3	1. Claim
	2. Evidence
	  • Appropriate
	  • Sufficient
	3. Reasoning
	  • Multiple components

Variation #4	1. Claim
	2. Evidence
	  • Appropriate
	  • Sufficient
	3. Reasoning
	  • Multiple components
	4. Rebuttal

increases. Finally, the fourth variation adds the rebuttal to the framework. Varying the level and degree of complexity can help you design assessment items that are appropriate for students with a range of experiences and prior knowledge.

In addition to the four different variations, you should also consider any common difficulties your students have with writing scientific explanations, such as including multiple pieces of evidence or only including appropriate evidence. In order to assess whether or not students have improved in this area, you can include one of the more challenging aspects in the assessment task. For example, if your students struggle with differentiating between appropriate and inappropriate evidence, include both types of evidence in the question to determine whether they can differentiate between the two. However, you also want to keep in mind that the assessment task should be appropriate for your students' current level of understanding, because they can become overwhelmed by complex tasks. In deciding on the level of complexity of the scientific explanation in the assessment item, consider the four different variations of the framework, the level of experience of your students, and the common difficulties of your students. In this way, you will design assessment tasks appropriate for your students.

Fifth-grade Food Web Case—Scientific Explanation Level of Complexity

For the fifth-grade students, we worked with Mr. Cardone to develop the assessment for an end-of-school-year test after they had been working with the framework over the course of the year. The target level for the assessment item was variation #2 in that students were expected to: (1) provide a claim, (2) provide evidence that was both appropriate and sufficient, and (3) provide reasoning that included scientific principles. Over the school year, Mr. Cardone focused on helping his students develop a stronger understanding of evidence. Consequently, he expected his students to include all appropriate evidence in their response so he wanted to develop an item that included multiple pieces of evidence. In terms of reasoning, this was an area that was still challenging for his fifth-grade students. He did expect students to use scientific principles, but he did not expect his students to write complex reasoning with multiple steps. Consequently, in the design of the assessment item and associated rubric we limited the complexity of the reasoning.

Seventh-grade Chemical Reaction Case—Scientific Explanation Level of Complexity

For the seventh-grade students, we developed the assessment as part of an end-of-unit test for a curriculum that included a focus on scientific explanation. During the curriculum, students had up to thirteen opportunities to write scientific explanations supported by curricular scaffolds and teaching strategies. The target level of the scientific explanation framework for this assessment item was variation #3. Students were expected to: (1) provide a claim, (2) provide evidence that was both appropriate and sufficient, and (3) provide reasoning that included scientific principles and multiple components to justify the claim. The level of reasoning for the seventh-graders was more complex and we expected them to discuss the scientific principle in more depth. Yet we did not expect the students to provide a rebuttal, because they had not been introduced to this component of the framework. If the students had been introduced to a rebuttal at this time, we would have designed both the assessment item and rubric to include the fourth component as well. In discussing this item, we will describe what modifications could be made in order to assess students for variation #4 of the framework, which does include the rebuttal.

Step 3: Create Learning Performances

Once the science content and scientific explanation have been unpacked, the next step is to combine the two in order to create a learning performance. A learning performance is a learning goal that goes beyond just stating the content knowledge; instead, a learning performance describes how students will be able to apply or use the science content knowledge (Krajcik, McNeill, & Reiser, 2008). In science, we want students to be able to use content knowledge in a variety of scientific practices such as designing an investigation, analyzing data, constructing scientific explanations, and building models. Specifically, in this book we focus on the scientific inquiry practice of constructing scientific explanations. In terms of designing assessment tasks that means the task needs to include data that students will analyze and use in their scientific explanation in which they justify their claim with evidence and reasoning. To develop a scientific explanation learning performance, we cross a science content standard with the scientific practice of constructing scientific explanations to create the learning performance. Developing a learning performance provides an explicit learning goal, which can then guide the design of both the assessment and the associated rubric, because it clearly states the expectations for the claim, evidence, reasoning, and rebuttal. The development of learning performances is also a key step that helps ensure alignment because it clearly specifies what you expect of your students.

Fifth-grade Food Web Case—Learning Performance

We previously described the key science concepts involved in the NRC grade 5–8 food web science standard. Figure 5.1 illustrates how that content standard can be combined with the science standards targeting scientific explanation to develop a learning performance that specifies a particular outcome. The goal is for students to go beyond just being able to define a food web or even to be able to look at a food web and state what the relationships are between different organisms. Instead, we want students to be able to use the data provided in a food web in terms of the

FIGURE 5.1
Food Web Learning Performance

Content Standard ×	Scientific Explanation = (scientific inquiry standards)	Learning Performance
"Populations of organisms can be categorized by the function they serve in an ecosystem. Plants and some micro-organisms are producers—they make their own food. All animals, including humans, are consumers, which obtain food by eating other organisms. Decomposers, primarily bacteria and fungi, are consumers that use waste materials and dead organisms for food. Food webs identify the relationships among producers, consumers, and decomposers in an ecosystem." (NRC, 1996, C: 4/2, 5–8)	"Develop . . . explanations . . . using evidence." (NRC, 1996, A: 1/4, 5–8) "Think critically and logically to make the relationships between evidence and explanation." (NRC, 1996, A: 1/4, 5–8)	Students construct a scientific explanation stating a claim about what will happen to the population size of an organism in a food web, providing evidence in the form of specific relationships in the food web and changes in population size of other organisms, and reasoning about how changing the population size of one organism impacts the population size of multiple other organisms in the food web, including both direct and indirect relationships.

relationships between organisms, as well as information about the population sizes of the organisms, to make a claim about how changes in the food web will affect different organisms.

The learning performance in Figure 5.1 specifically states that students will make a claim about what will happen to the population size of an organism in a food web, will provide evidence in the form of specific relationships in the food web and changes in the population size of other organisms along with reasoning about how changing the population size of one organism impacts the population size of multiple other organisms in the food web, including both direct and indirect relationships. This learning performance specifies what we would like students to be able to do in terms of using their understanding of food webs combined with their understanding of scientific explanations. Learning performances move beyond students memorizing facts to illustrating what it looks like for students to do science. The level of specificity of the learning performance is critical for ensuring alignment with the assessment task.

Seventh-grade Chemical Reaction Case—Learning Performance

Similar to the food web learning performance, the chemical reaction learning performance combines the learning goals around scientific explanation and chemical reactions to specify what students should be able to do with that knowledge. Although we do want students to be able to define what a chemical reaction is, we also want them to go beyond defining to be able to construct a claim about whether or not a chemical reaction has occurred during a particular situation and to justify their claim. Figure 5.2 illustrates how we combined the chemical reaction content standard with the scientific explanation inquiry standards to develop the learning performance.

The chemical reaction learning performance states that students construct scientific explanations stating a claim whether a chemical reaction occurred, evidence in the form of properties for the different substances, and reasoning that a chemical reaction is a process in which old substances interact to form new substances with different properties compared to the old substances. If we included the rebuttal in the assessment item, we would expand the learning performance to add a statement about the rebuttal: *a rebuttal that the process is not a mixture or a phase change because a mixture is just a combination of the old substances and a phase change is the same substance in a different state.* Students should be able to apply their understanding of chemical reactions to analyze data and determine whether a chemical reaction has occurred. Learning performances go beyond providing statements

FIGURE 5.2
Chemical Reaction Learning Performance

Content Standard	×	Scientific Explanation (scientific inquiry standards)	=	Learning Performance
"Substances react chemically in characteristic ways with other substances to form new substances with different characteristic properties." (AAAS, 2008, 4D/M11**)		"Develop . . . explanations . . . using evidence." (NRC, 1996, A: 1/4, 5–8) "Think critically and logically to make the relationships between evidence and explanation." (NRC, 1996, A: 1/5, 5–8)		Students construct scientific explanations stating a claim whether a chemical reaction occurred, evidence in the form of properties for the different substances, and reasoning that a chemical reaction is a process in which old substances interact to form new substances with different properties compared to the old substances.

of content knowledge to specifying what students should be able to do with that knowledge—how they should use that knowledge to construct evidence-based explanations about the world around them.

Step 4: Write the Assessment Task

The previous three steps in the development process lay important foundation for designing scientific explanation assessment tasks that target the key science content as well as align with the appropriate variation of the scientific explanation framework for your students. The process of unpacking the content provides you with the content to embed in the question as well as any common student difficulties with the content to include in the item. Selecting the level of complexity for scientific explanation provides insight into the number of components and the level of complexity you want to target in terms of the framework. Developing the learning performances provides a clear goal for the outcome of the assessment task in terms of combining the content and scientific explanation and provides specific guidance about what students should be including in their writing for an assessment task. In addition to considering the first three steps, writing the assessment item requires identifying a context that is accessible to students. The context determines the specific phenomenon addressed in the question and the data students analyze in order to construct and justify their claim. The context is important because, as we discuss in the two cases, students are not writing about a scientific concept in general (e.g., food webs); rather, they are applying what they know about the scientific concept to make sense of a specific example or phenomenon (e.g., a food web for a coniferous forest).

Fifth-grade Food Web Case—Assessment Task

In terms of the content in the food web assessment item, we want to target students' understanding of the relationships between organisms, including evaluating whether students hold the common alternative conception that indirect relationships in food webs do not impact population size. In terms of the level of complexity of scientific explanation, we target the second variation of the framework. The learning performance clarifies that we want students to make a claim about what happens to one organism when the population size of another organism changes. Finally, in terms of the context, we select organisms local to the area where the fifth-graders live to increase their potential familiarity with the terms in the food web. Based on this groundwork, we wrote the assessment item in Figure 5.3.

Since we developed the question for fifth-graders, we kept the food web relatively simple, including only seven organisms. But we were interested in indirect relationships, so we specifically included some in the food web. We also worded the question to ask about the hawk and the seed, which are not directly linked to each other, in order to evaluate the students' understanding of this indirect relationship.

FIGURE 5.3

Food Web Assessment Task

Examine the food web below:

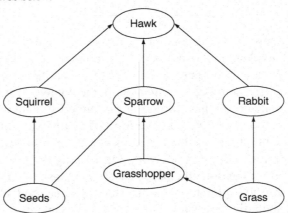

Write a scientific argument that answers the following question: What would happen to the size of the hawk population if all the seeds were removed from the ecosystem? Remember to support your claim with evidence and reasoning.

Including the indirect links will help us assess whether students hold common alternative conceptions that if the population size of one organism in a food web changes, it will only impact other organisms that are directly linked to that organism. We developed this question for Mr. Cardone's classroom, who referred to the claim, evidence, and reasoning framework as a scientific argument. Consequently, the phrase "scientific argument" is used in the question. Furthermore, he felt his students still needed support in developing arguments, so we included the prompt: *Remember to support your claim with evidence and reasoning* to help students link back to their prior experiences in class developing arguments in both writing and talk. This food web combines the information from steps 1–3 in a context that is accessible to the fifth-grade students.

Seventh-grade Chemical Reaction Case—Assessment Task

For the chemical reaction scientific explanation assessment item, the unpacking of the content standard specifies the key science concept that a chemical reaction is a process where new substances are made from old substances. We also include the potential student alternative conception that students have difficulty understanding what characteristics count as properties to differentiate one substance from another substance. In terms of the level of complexity of scientific explanation, our expectation is for students to write a scientific explanation at variation #3 without any prompting about the framework. The learning performance specifies what we would be looking for in the student writing. Finally, for the context we selected a real chemical reaction that included changes in properties that students learned about during the chemistry unit. Based on this work, we developed the scientific explanation assessment item in Figure 5.4.

Since the content is more complicated and the expectations for students are more complex, we made several decisions in designing the assessment to make it challenging for seventh-grade students. In designing the assessment item, we purposefully included multiple pieces of data in both the text and in the table in order to increase the complexity by including both appropriate and inappropriate evidence as well as to assess for students' alternative conceptions. For example, we included *volume* as one of the measurements, because this is one of the characteristics students

FIGURE 5.4

Chemical Reaction Assessment Task

Carlos wants to know if two liquids will react with each other. He uses an eyedropper to get a sample from the two liquids—butanic acid and butanol. He takes some measurements of each of the two samples. Then he stirs the two liquids together and heats them. After stirring and heating the liquids, they form two separate layers—layer A and layer B. Carlos uses an eyedropper to get a sample from each layer. He takes some measurements of each sample. Here are his results:

		Measurements			
		Melting Point	Volume	Solubility in Water	Density
Before stirring & heating	Sample of butanic acid	–7.9 °C	2.00 cm³	Yes	0.96 g/cm³
	Sample of butanol	–89.5 °C	2.00 cm³	Yes	0.81 g/cm³
After stirring & heating	Sample of layer A	–91.5 °C	2.00 cm³	No	0.87 g/cm³
	Sample of layer B	0.0 °C	2.00 cm³	Yes	1.00 g/cm³

Write a **scientific explanation** that states whether a chemical reaction occurred when Carlos stirred and heated butanic acid and butanol.

can incorrectly focus on instead of examining properties that are independent of the amount of the sample to determine whether or not two samples are the same substance. The reasoning is also more complex because students need to know and articulate both that a chemical reaction produces new substances and what properties count as evidence to determine whether or not the substances before versus after stirring and heating are the same or different. Consequently, this second example requires a more sophisticated response than the fifth-grade food web scientific explanation assessment task. Yet we designed both assessment items with both the student audience in mind as well as the content and scientific explanation learning goals for this particular task.

If students have learned about rebuttals, this item could be modified to support the inclusion of this component in students' responses. For example, changing the wording of the last sentence opens up the question to include the possibility of multiple claims: *Write a **scientific explanation** that states what process occurred when Carlos stirred and heated butanic acid and butanol.* In classrooms where the norm is for students to always include a rebuttal in their writing, they would explain not only why they think one process did occur (e.g., chemical reaction), but also why they believe other processes did *not* occur (e.g., phase change). If students are new at providing rebuttals, the last sentence could also provide more explicit support to remind students to include a rebuttal in their response: *Write a **scientific explanation** that states what process (chemical reaction, mixing, or phase change) occurred when Carlos stirred and heated butanic acid and butanol. Include in your explanation why you did **not** select the other two processes as your claim.* The second wording provides explicit support for students to include the rebuttal in their response. The decision of whether or not to require a rebuttal as well as how much support to provide students in the prompt depends on the age and experience of your students.

Step 5: Review the Assessment Task

After writing the assessment task, we then evaluate the task by using an assessment evaluation framework developed by Project 2061 (DeBoer, 2005). The Project 2061 assessment evaluation framework uses three questions:

(1) Is the knowledge needed to correctly respond to the task?

(2) Is the knowledge enough by itself to correctly respond to the task or is additional knowledge needed?

(3) Is the assessment task and context likely to be comprehensible to students?

We refer to these as the necessity, sufficiency, and comprehensibility criteria.

The necessity criterion examines the alignment to make sure the assessment task focuses on the knowledge in the content and inquiry goals specified by the designers. In order to respond appropriately to the assessment items, students need to have that knowledge in those goals. Sometimes students can get the correct answer for a question by using test-taking skills instead of applying their understanding of the science content. Steps 1–3 in our assessment development process help support us in this alignment to make sure knowledge of the content and scientific explanation are necessary to correctly respond to the question.

The sufficiency criterion examines whether other content knowledge, beyond what is specified in the learning goals, is required to answer the question. Sometimes the "other content knowledge" can include ideas that students have previously learned, and it is appropriate to include them in the assessment item. At other times, the "other content knowledge" can include ideas that go beyond the desired learning goal and you would not expect students to know, in which case the question would need to be revised in order to focus the scope of the assessment. The sufficiency criterion helps you consider what other knowledge is included in the item and whether or not that other knowledge is appropriate.

The comprehensibility criterion takes into consideration the prior experiences and cultural backgrounds of the students as well as the literacy demands of the task. This criterion helps to ensure that the assessment item is appropriately written to meet the experiences and background knowledge of your students. For example, if you are writing assessment items for students in Texas, you do not want to focus on snow skiing as the context of the question. The students may have difficulty understanding the context so they are not able to appropriately show what they know about the science content. Furthermore, it is important to consider the reading demands of the question and whether or not they are appropriate for the student audience. After we write a scientific explanation assessment item, we use these three questions to reflect on the assessment item and evaluate the quality of the item.

Fifth-grade Food Web Case—Review

In considering the necessity criterion, students do need to understand the effects of both direct and indirect relationships in food webs to construct the correct claim that the size of the hawk population would decrease if all the seeds were removed from the ecosystem. In particular, if a student did not understand indirect relationships in food webs, they may incorrectly assume that the hawk population would remain the same because hawks do not eat seeds. The sufficiency criterion asks if other knowledge is needed to correctly answer the question. To correctly answer the question, students would not need to know conceptual understandings beyond the standard. Students would need to understand food webs as well as a basic understanding of ecosystems, both of which were included in the unpacking of the standard (see Table 5.2). Furthermore, students need to understand how to support the claim they are making with the appropriate evidence and reasoning. This knowledge about food webs and scientific explanation aligns with our goals for the assessment item. The last Project 2061 criterion addresses whether or not the question would be comprehensible to students. This question was written for fifth-grade students in a large urban school district in the northeastern United States. The organisms in the ecosystem were selected because they all live in that area of the country. If the question was being used with different students in another area of the country or in a different country, other organisms may need to be substituted to align with the local ecosystems. The literacy level of the question is appropriate for fifth-grade students. The more complex terms in the question, such as food web, scientific argument, and ecosystem, were all extensively discussed in their science class.

Seventh-grade Chemical Reaction Case—Review

In terms of the necessity criterion, the science content knowledge about chemical reactions is needed to correctly respond to this question. To correctly construct and justify the claim that a chemical reaction did occur, students would need to understand that layers A and B are different substances than butanic acid and butanol, because their properties (melting point, solubility, and density) are different. This idea aligns with the key science concepts in the unpacking of the science standard. In terms of the sufficiency criterion, besides understanding chemical reactions and scientific explanations, a student would also need to understand how to read a data table. If students had a challenging time interpreting data tables, they would have difficulty with this assessment task. Reading a data table is another key aspect of science. Consequently, although this goes beyond the explicit goals in the learning performance, we decided to keep the data as presented in a data table because the seventh-grade students had previously learned how to interpret data tables. Finally, in terms of whether the question would be comprehensible to seventh-grade students, the literacy demands of the question are challenging. The question includes a lot of text as well as information in the data table. In designing the assessment task, we wanted to design a more complex scientific explanation assessment item for the students, because they had been provided with a variety of support and practice in their science classrooms. If the students were less experienced with scientific explanation, it probably would have been more appropriate to design a less challenging item for the students.

Step 6: Develop a Specific Rubric

Once the assessment item aligns with the key content and scientific explanation learning goals as well as meets the Project 2061 criteria, we then develop a specific rubric for the assessment item. The two examples in this chapter illustrate how to develop rubrics for assessment tasks, but you can also develop rubrics for learning tasks using the same process. The scientific explanations students construct during learning tasks can be used as either formative or summative assessments to inform your own instruction and to assess the quality of student work.

We design the specific rubric by adapting a base rubric that can be used across any science content area or context (McNeill & Krajcik, 2008b; McNeill, Lizotte, Krajcik, & Marx, 2006). Table 5.5 provides the base scientific explanation rubric, which includes the four different components of the framework, and provides guidance for thinking about those components in terms of different levels of student achievement. In considering the quality of the claim, evidence, reasoning, and rebuttal we consider the appropriateness and sufficiency for each component in relation to the assessment question with each level representing increased sophistication in the students' response. When we adapt the base rubric to develop the specific rubric, we align the rubric with the particular assessment task. A student not only needs to include claim, evidence, reasoning, and rebuttal in their response, but each of these components needs to be scientifically accurate and specifically address the question or problem being asked.

We often begin by writing an ideal student response for the assessment task to make explicit our expectations about what students should include in the response in terms of the quantity and complexity of the different components. We use this ideal response in conjunction with the base rubric to develop the specific rubric. The development of the specific rubric determines how many components are included (e.g., may not include rebuttal), the levels for each component (e.g., a response may only require two pieces of evidence), and the specific content included for each component (e.g., what counts as reasoning for a specific assessment item). The base rubric provides guidance, yet specific rubrics can look quite different from one another depending on the complexity of the item and the expectations for students. A specific rubric can include three components and two levels for each component (max score of 6), four components and four levels for each component (max score of 16), or three components and have different levels for each component such as two levels for claim, four levels for evidence, and three levels for reasoning (max score of 9). We return to the food web and chemical reaction cases to illustrate how to develop the specific rubrics.

Fifth-grade Food Web Example—Specific Rubric

In developing the specific rubric for the food web assessment, we only include the three components (claim, evidence, and reasoning) that we specified students include in the assessment item. We then write an ideal student response to illustrate our expectations for each of these components:

> *The hawk population would decrease (CLAIM). The hawk eats rabbit, sparrow, and squirrel. The squirrel only eats seeds, so without seeds there will no longer be squirrels. The sparrow eats grasshoppers and seeds, so there will be fewer sparrows. The rabbits do not eat seeds, so there will be the same amount (EVIDENCE). Organisms are affected by other organisms in a food web even if they are not directly linked to them. There will be fewer hawks, because they will have less food to eat (REASONING).*

TABLE 5.5 Base Rubric for Scientific Explanation

LEVEL	Claim	Evidence	Reasoning	Rebuttal
	A statement or conclusion that answers the original question/problem.	*Scientific data that supports the claim. The data needs to be appropriate and sufficient to support the claim.*	*A justification that connects the evidence to the claim. It shows why the data counts as evidence by using appropriate and sufficient scientific principles.*	*Recognizes and describes alternative explanations, and provides counter evidence and reasoning for why the alternative explanation is not appropriate.*
0	Does not make a claim, or makes an inaccurate claim.	Does not provide evidence, or only provides inappropriate evidence (evidence that does not support claim).	Does not provide reasoning, or only provides inappropriate reasoning.	Does not recognize that an alternative explanation exists and does not provide a rebuttal or makes an inaccurate rebuttal.
Varies from 1 to 5	Makes an accurate but incomplete claim.	Provides appropriate, but insufficient, evidence to support claim. May include some inappropriate evidence.	Provides reasoning that connects the evidence to the claim. May include some scientific principles or justification for why the evidence supports the claim, but not sufficiently.	Recognizes alternative explanations and provides appropriate but insufficient counter evidence and reasoning in making a rebuttal.
	Makes an accurate and complete claim.	Provides appropriate and sufficient evidence to support claim.	Provides reasoning that connects the evidence to the claim. Includes appropriate and sufficient scientific principles to explain why the evidence supports the claim.	Recognizes alternative explanations and provides appropriate and sufficient counter evidence and reasoning when making rebuttals.

114

The ideal student response allows us to consider how many different levels to include in each of the three components (see Table 5.6).

Claim. For the claim, we include three different levels for the student response. The highest level for claim for this assessment task is a Level 2 in which a student provides an accurate and complete claim that the hawk population will decrease. Level 1 includes an accurate but incomplete or vague claim such as the hawk population will change, without specifying that it will decrease. Level 0 includes an inaccurate claim such as a student responding that the hawk population will not change.

Evidence. For evidence, students can receive five possible scores that range from level 0 to level 4. We were interested to see if the students would discuss all the information they used as evidence to construct their claim. The highest score, a level 4, includes four different pieces of evidence in the student's response: (1) hawks eat rabbits, sparrows, and squirrels, (2) squirrels only eat seeds so without seeds there will be no squirrels, (3) sparrows eat seeds and grasshoppers so there will be fewer sparrows, and (4) rabbits do not eat seeds so there will be the same amount. These four different pieces of evidence articulate the data implicit in the food web representation that a student needs to consider to determine what would happen to the hawk population. A student receives a level 3 if they talked about three of these pieces of evidence, a level 2 if they talk about two of these pieces of evidence, and a level 1 if they only talk about one piece of evidence. Finally, a student receives a level 0 for evidence if they either do not provide any evidence or if they provide only inappropriate evidence in terms of the relationships between the different organisms and how removing the seeds would impact their population size.

Reasoning. In assessing the students' reasoning, we examine how well they use scientific principles in order to develop a justification for why their evidence supports their claim. For this assessment task, because it focuses on indirect relationships, students need to include in their reasoning an articulation of their inferences for why altering one population in the food web is going to impact the other organisms even if they do not directly eat those organisms. We developed the rubric to include three different potential levels for students' reasoning ranging from level 0 to level 2. In order to receive the highest score of a level 2, students need to include the following two aspects: (1) Organisms are affected by indirect relationships in food webs. (2) There will be fewer hawks because it will have less food to eat. The reasoning includes two key aspects. First, students need to realize that indirect relationships can affect the size of a population. Using this knowledge, students can then determine that the hawk population will decrease, because one of the hawk's food sources (i.e., squirrels) will disappear and another food source (i.e., sparrows) will decrease. A student also has to determine that the hawk population

TABLE 5.6 Specific Rubric for Food Web Assessment

	Claim	Evidence	Reasoning
	A statement or conclusion that answers the original question/problem.	*Scientific data that supports the claim. The data need to be appropriate and sufficient to support the claim.*	*A justification that connects the evidence to the claim. It shows why the data count as evidence by using appropriate and sufficient scientific principles.*
0	Does not make a claim, or makes an inaccurate claim. States that the hawk population will not change.	Does not provide evidence, or only provides inappropriate evidence (evidence that does not support claim). Provides inappropriate data, like "rabbits don't eat sparrows," or provides vague evidence, like "the arrows are my evidence."	Does not provide reasoning, or only provides reasoning that does not link evidence to claim. Provides an inappropriate reasoning statement, like "the hawk is not impacted by the seeds," or does not provide any reasoning.
1	Makes an accurate, but incomplete claim. States that the hawk population will change.	Provides 1 of the following 4 pieces of evidence: • Hawks eat rabbit, sparrow, and squirrel • Squirrels only eat seeds so there will no longer be squirrels • Sparrows eat seeds and grasshoppers so there will be fewer sparrows • Rabbits do not eat seeds so there will be the same amount May also include inappropriate evidence.	Provides incomplete reasoning that includes 1 of 2 aspects: • Organisms are affected by indirect relationships in food webs • There will be fewer hawks because it will have less food to eat
2	Makes an accurate and complete claim. States that the hawk population will decrease.	Provides 2 of the following 4 pieces of evidence: • Hawk eats rabbit, sparrow, and squirrel • Squirrel only eats seeds so there will no longer be squirrels • Sparrow eats seeds and grasshoppers so there will be fewer sparrows • Rabbits do not eat seeds so there will be the same amount May also include inappropriate evidence.	Provides complete reasoning that includes the following 2 aspects: • Organisms are affected by indirect relationships in food webs • There will be fewer hawks because it will have less food to eat
3		Provides 3 of the following 4 pieces of evidence: • Hawk eats rabbit, sparrow, and squirrel • Squirrel only eats seeds so there will no longer be squirrels • Sparrow eats seeds and grasshoppers so there will be fewer sparrows • Rabbits do not eat seeds so there will be the same amount May also include inappropriate evidence.	
4		Provides all 4 of the following pieces of evidence: • Hawk eats rabbit, sparrow, and squirrel • Squirrel only eats seeds so there will no longer be squirrels • Sparrow eats seeds and grasshoppers so there will be fewer sparrows • Rabbits do not eat seeds so there will be the same amount It does not include any inappropriate evidence.	

will not end up at zero, because there is still some food available for the hawk (i.e., some sparrows and rabbits). If a student describes one of these two aspects, they receive a level 1. A level 0 for reasoning is if a student provides no reasoning or only inappropriate reasoning.

In developing the rubric for this assessment item, we could also envision more detailed and complex reasoning included in the student writing. Instead of just including the two sentences in our ideal response, a student could articulate more detailed reasoning such as: *Organisms are affected by other organisms in a food web even if they are not directly linked to them. Although the hawk does not eat seeds, it eats sparrows and squirrels that eat seeds. Since the sparrow will decrease and there will no longer be squirrels to eat, the hawk population will decrease. But there will still be some hawks, because they will still have some sparrows and all the rabbits to eat.* Although this detailed reasoning would be more complete, it was not our expectation that the fifth-grade students would include this much information. Rather, we designed the rubric such that the highest level aligned with our goal for these particular students. There are always tradeoffs in designing rubrics in terms of how much detail to include and how complex to make the highest level. If we designed this rubric for older or more experienced students, we would include more levels in the reasoning. When designing rubrics for your students, you will often be confronted with multiple choices and will need to decide based on what you think is appropriate for your students.

Seventh-grade Chemical Reaction Example—Specific Rubric

In developing the specific rubric for the seventh-grade chemical reaction assessment, we went through a similar process. As with the food web example, this assessment requires that students include three components in their response (claim, evidence, and reasoning) though in this item they were not explicitly prompted to include those elements. We began by developing an ideal student response:

> *A chemical reaction did occur (CLAIM). Butanic acid and butanol have different solubilities compared to layer A and layer B. Butanic acid and butanol also have different melting points and densities compared to the measurements for layer A and layer B (EVIDENCE). The volume is not important, because it is not a property. Properties are characteristics of a substance that are independent of the amount of the sample such as solubility, density, and melting point. Since the properties are different, layers A and B are new substances, because different substances have different properties. A chemical reaction occurred, because new substances were created from old substances (REASONING).*

The ideal student response clearly specifies what to look for in students' claim, evidence, and reasoning. We want students to justify that a chemical reaction has occurred using the appropriate data from the assessment task as well as providing their reasoning for why they used that particular evidence and why that evidence supports their claim.

Claim. Table 5.7 includes the rubric we developed for this assessment item. Because of how the science assessment was worded (i.e., Write a scientific explanation that states whether a chemical reaction occurred when Carlos stirred and heated butanic acid and butanol), there are only two potential claims that a student can construct. Students can either write that a chemical reaction did occur or that a chemical reaction did not occur. Consequently, for claim there are only two different levels for a student response either a level 0 or a level 1. Students who state that a chemical reaction did occur receive a level 1 and those students that did not make a claim or make an inappropriate claim receive a level 0.

Evidence. For evidence, there are three pieces of evidence that students need to include in their response resulting in four different levels ranging from level 0 to level 3. The three pieces of evidence include: (1) Butanic acid and butanol have different solubilities compared to layer A and layer B. (2) Butanic acid and butanol have different melting points compared to layer A and layer B. (3) Butanic acid and butanol have different densities compared to layer A and layer B. It is important not only that the students talk about solubility, melting point, and density as being different, but also that they compare the before (butanic acid and butanol) and after (layer A and layer B) pairs of liquids. If students talk about butanic acid and butanol having different densities or layers A and layers B having different densities, this is actually not appropriate evidence to determine whether or not a chemical reaction occurred. The important comparison to make is before and after stirring and heating.

Similar to the previous food web rubric, we made choices when designing this rubric in terms of how much detail to include. In terms of evidence, some teachers require their students to include the actual numbers or observations in their scientific explanation when they discuss the data. The inclusion of specific numbers could be added to the evidence component of the rubric, which could add an additional level to the rubric (level 4). The level of detail in the evidence is dependent on your specific expectations for your students.

Reasoning. Finally, for reasoning, students need to describe why this particular evidence is important to determine whether a chemical reaction occurred and why they did not include other data as evidence. Students need to include in their response the following: (1) A chemical reaction creates new substances from old substances. (2) Different substances have different properties. (3) Properties are

TABLE 5.7 Specific Rubric for Chemical Reaction Scientific Explanation Assessment

	Claim	Evidence	Reasoning
	A statement or conclusion that answers the original question/problem.	*Scientific data that supports the claim. The data need to be appropriate and sufficient to support the claim.*	*A justification that connects the evidence to the claim. It shows why the data count as evidence by using appropriate and sufficient scientific principles.*
0	Does not make a claim, or makes an inaccurate claim. States that a chemical reaction did not occur.	Does not provide evidence, or only provides inappropriate evidence (evidence that does not support claim). Provides only inappropriate data, like "Carlos heated and stirred the liquids," or provides vague evidence, like "the data shows me it is true."	Does not provide reasoning, or only provides reasoning that does not link evidence to claim. Provides an inappropriate reasoning statement, like "a chemical reaction did not occur because Layers A and B are not substances," or does not provide any reasoning.
1	Makes an accurate and complete claim. States that a chemical reaction did occur.	Provides 1 of the following 3 pieces of evidence: • Butanic acid and butanol have different solubilities compared to layer A and B • Butanic acid and butanol have different melting points compared to layer A and B • Butanic acid and butanol have different densities compared to layer A and B May also include inappropriate evidence, like volume, stirring, or heating.	Provides 1 of the following 3 reasoning components: • A chemical reaction creates new or different substances • Different substances have different properties. • Properties are characteristics of a substance that are independent of the amount of the sample (solubility, density, and melting point) and volume is not a property
2		Provides 2 of the following 3 pieces of evidence: • Butanic acid and butanol have different solubilities compared to layer A and B • Butanic acid and butanol have different melting points compared to layer A and B • Butanic acid and butanol have different densities compared to layer A and B May also include inappropriate evidence, like volume, stirring, or heating.	Provides 2 of the following 3 reasoning components: • A chemical reaction creates new or different substances • Different substances have different properties • Properties are characteristics of a substance that are independent of the amount of the sample (solubility, density, and melting point) and volume is not a property
3		Provides all 3 of the following pieces of evidence: • Butanic acid and butanol have different solubilities compared to layer A and B • Butanic acid and butanol have different melting points compared to layer A and B • Butanic acid and butanol have different densities compared to layer A and B It does not include any inappropriate evidence.	Provides all 3 reasoning components: • A chemical reaction creates new or different substances • Different substances have different properties • Properties are characteristics of a substance that are independent of the amount of the sample (solubility, density, and melting point) and volume is not a property

119

characteristics of a substance that are independent of the amount of the sample (solubility, density, and melting point) and volume is not a property.

The students need to describe the general science principle in terms of what occurs during a chemical reaction and how they use their understanding of the scientific principles to make sense of the data. The reasoning should articulate how they use the information for solubility, density, and melting point to determine that there were new substances created, which is how they knew a chemical reaction occurred. The reasoning should also explain why they did not use volume as evidence for whether a chemical reaction occurred.

Rebuttal. With different student expectations and wording of the question, students can also be required to include a rebuttal in their scientific explanation for this assessment item. Students can make a case for why, when Carlos stirred and heated the two liquids, he did not cause a phase change or a mixture. For example, the ideal student response could include the following rebuttal: *Another explanation could be that a mixture was created or a third explanation could be that a phase change occurred. Since there is a new substance, it cannot be a mixture or a phase change. A mixture would just be a combination of the old substances and a phase change would be the same substance in a different state.* This rebuttal includes two different key ideas: (1) the process was not a mixture, because mixtures just combine old substances, and (2) the process was not a phase change, because phase changes are the same substance in a different state. Consequently, if the rebuttal were added to the rubric, it would consist of three levels (Level 0, Level 1, and Level 2) depending on how many of the key ideas students discuss. If you use this item with more experienced students, including this rebuttal is an appropriate expectation for their responses.

Developing specific rubrics for assessment items explicitly articulates what you are looking for in students' responses for their claim, evidence, reasoning, and, potentially, rebuttal. The specific rubric combines both the general framework of scientific explanation with the content and context of the assessment task. Students need to not only include evidence and reasoning to support their claims, but that justification needs to be scientifically accurate. Specific rubrics help guide you in pushing your student use of evidence and reasoning to a deeper level. The details of the specific rubric will depend on your expectations for your students. As we discussed with the two example cases, if these items were given to older or more experienced students you may want students to include more complex reasoning or a rebuttal in their scientific explanations. These two cases just illustrate how to develop specific rubrics, but as you incorporate these strategies into your classroom, you will need to adapt them to make them most effective for your students.

In this chapter, we described our six-step process for designing scientific explanation assessment items:

(1) Identify and unpack content standard

(2) Select scientific explanation level of complexity

(3) Create learning performance

(4) Write assessment task

(5) Review assessment task

(6) Develop specific rubric

Using this process allows us to develop assessment items that target the key learning goals around both the science content and scientific explanations and ensures that you are designing assessment items appropriate for the background experiences and prior knowledge of all your students. Furthermore, they allow us to assess whether or not students struggle with potential alternative concepts either around the science content or scientific explanation. In the next chapter, we will focus on how you can use the rubrics and student data to assess your students' current level of understanding and then adapt your instruction to best meet their needs. In the final Chapter 7, we discuss how to better support student learning over time, whether your focus is on one year in your classroom or if supporting scientific explanations is a district level goal across multiple years.

Study Group Questions

1. How is unpacking a content standard different compared to the process that you typically use to develop science assessments? What are the benefits and disadvantages of going through this process?
2. Select a standard for your science curriculum and create an assessment task using the six steps for the development process.
   a. Why did you select the scientific explanation level of complexity for your specific assessment task?
   b. Give the assessment task to a colleague and ask them to write an ideal student response. How is your colleague's student response different from the one you wrote? Why do you think it is different? Does it suggest the need for any potential revisions to the assessment item?
3. How are the specific rubrics different from the rubrics you have used in your science classroom in the past? What are the benefits and disadvantages of these rubrics?

6

Using Rubrics and Student Data to Inform Instruction

What insights do students' scientific explanations provide you about student thinking? How can your assessment of students' scientific explanation inform your own instruction? How can you provide students with feedback to support them in developing a stronger understanding of both scientific explanations and the science content? Let's consider the following vignette that shows how an eighth-grade science teacher uses the assessment of his students' work to inform and modify his instruction.

Mr. Glosser, an eighth-grade science teacher, has his students conduct an experiment to determine the amount of chemical energy stored in different food molecules. His class burns 3 grams of commercially purchased vegetable oil and 3 grams of marshmallow and compares how much energy is released by heating 30 mL of water. He instructs his class to write a scientific explanation that answers the question: Does vegetable oil or marshmallow contain more food energy?

Sarah and Josh collect the following data:

Substance burned (3 grams)	Water temperature *before* heating (°C)	Water temperature *after* heating (°C)	*Change* in water Temperature (°C)
Vegetable Oil	22	69	47
Marshmallow	21	27	6

They then use their data to write the following scientific explanation:

> *The vegetable oil contains more energy per gram than marshmallows. Our evidence for this is that burning vegetable oil increased the water temperature more than burning the same amount of marshmallows. The vegetable oil raised the water 47°C and the marshmallows raised it 6°C. Because the oil raised the water temperature more than the marshmallows did, the oil has more energy than the marshmallow.*

Mr. Glosser uses his rubric to guide the scoring of their response. Although Mr. Glosser is pleased that Sarah and Josh's explanation includes a claim and evidence, he is disappointed that they did not describe the scientific principles as part of their reasoning. He was hoping they would say that when a substance burns, the chemical energy is converted to thermal energy and the thermal energy is transferred to the water so the water molecules move faster and result in a temperature increase.

Mr. Glosser continues to score other students' scientific explanations in his class. Although many of his students make an appropriate claim, less of them provide appropriate evidence and most do not include the reasoning he had hoped. Here is a quote from Mr. Glosser:

> *By looking at their writing, I was able to see where they were having a hard time and it was a little frustrating. They had a hard time specifically with the reasoning—the reasoning part was definitely the hardest, but also just the whole idea of writing out an explanation was hard for them. They're definitely used to writing fill in the blank, or doing multiple choice, so it's hard for them to actually write a coherent paragraph, particularly in science.*

Although Mr. Glosser hoped to move on to the next lesson in the unit, based on the scoring of the scientific explanations, he decides that the next day in class he needs to address both the evidence and scientific reasoning components of the explanation including readdressing some of the key science concepts. He decides that he will first lead a discussion to review what they learned about energy conversions and energy transfer. He also wants to

124

Using
Rubrics and
Student Data
to Inform
Instruction

review the idea that chemical bonds contain energy that can be converted to thermal energy during a chemical reaction such as burning. He will then have student groups critique each other's explanations and provide feedback on the claim, evidence, and reasoning components. Finally, each group will rewrite their explanations based on the feedback they receive from the class discussions and peer review.

This vignette illustrates how a teacher analyzed student writing to identify students' strengths and weaknesses. Using the results of students' work can provide valuable information for your instruction and how you might modify the instruction to improve student learning. In this chapter, we explore how you can use rubrics to make students' thinking visible to assess students' strengths and weaknesses as well as inform your own instruction. Analyzing student work and providing students supportive feedback can help all your students develop more thorough understandings of science content and the practice of writing scientific explanations. We examine a number of examples of student writing in order to illustrate this process. We also describe different types of feedback that can be provided to students in order to support them in greater student learning.

Role of Assessment in Creating a Supportive Learning Environment

Assessment can play multiple roles in the science classroom. In particular, assessments are characterized as either formative or summative assessments. Formative assessments provide information to teachers and students that are used to improve teaching and learning (NRC, 2001). Summative assessments are cumulative assessments that capture the quality of student learning and judge performance against some standard (NRC, 2001). You can often use the same assessment as both a formative and summative assessment measure. Traditionally, assessments have been viewed primarily for evaluation, but they can in fact play a much more dynamic role in classroom instruction in helping to diagnose student learning difficulties and in informing instruction. Encouraging student expression and defense of their ideas in science can not only make student thinking visible to the teacher, but it can also help students become aware of their own science ideas (Black, 2003). The process of writing, critiquing, and revising scientific explanations can support student learning in that it can be used to encourage student reflection on their understanding of science concepts. Students can be encouraged to reflect on questions such as: How are you making sense of the natural world around you? How are you applying science concepts to construct and justify claims? Encouraging students to reflect on these questions can provide greater self-awareness of their own understanding and ability to apply science concepts.

Using Assessments to Modify Instruction

125

Role of
Assessment
in Creating
a Supportive
Learning
Environment

Assessments are also essential tools to support teachers' efforts to improve instruction (Michaels, Shouse, & Schweingruber, 2008). Using assessments to gain insight into student thinking can result in teachers not only modifying their teaching approach or strategies, but can also change or add new teaching objectives to their future instruction (Sneider, 2003). Examining student work can reveal challenges you may not have originally realized that your students struggled with in their thinking or writing. Consequently, in order to support students in learning you may need to add an additional lesson or change an existing lesson to address a particular science concept or to help students understand how to provide reasoning or rebuttals for the claims they make. This is a very powerful technique to support all your students in learning science concepts and writing scientific explanations. For example, in the vignette about Mr. Glosser and his eighth-grade students, after reviewing their scientific explanations he realized he needed to add another lesson to review energy conversions and energy transfer as well as provide students with peer support and feedback in order to rewrite their scientific explanations to include stronger scientific reasoning.

Providing Students with Feedback

Teachers can also use assessment to provide their students with feedback about their performance. Using assessments to provide feedback turns assessments into valuable tools to promote student learning. Specific and descriptive feedback that focuses on both students' successes and ways to improve student work has a positive effect on student learning (Davies, 2003) and can support English language learners in acquiring a deeper understanding of both content and language skills (Echevarria, Vogt, & Short, 2008). This type of feedback can encourage student reflection and support greater student achievement on future work. In providing either written or spoken feedback, comments should be explicit and clear, point out strengths and weaknesses, provide suggestions on how to improve the scientific explanation, and ask questions to promote deeper student thinking. In providing students with feedback on their scientific explanations, we suggest providing comments on three different aspects: (1) inclusion and quality of the claim, evidence, reasoning, and, potentially, the rebuttal, (2) accuracy and thoroughness of the science content, and (3) holistic quality of the scientific explanation. For the first aspect, it is important to provide specific feedback on the different components in order to provide students with a sense of their strengths as well as a knowledge of the areas in which they need to improve. For example, in the vignette, Mr. Glosser would want to provide Sarah and Josh with feedback that their claim was correct and that they provided clear and detailed evidence to support their claim, but that he would like them to expand on their reasoning. He could ask probing questions—Why does the increase in temperature tell you that the

126

Using
Rubrics and
Student Data
to Inform
Instruction

oil has more energy? What is occurring to cause that increase in temperature?—in order to encourage students to reflect on how they could improve their reasoning. The second aspect focuses on the science content in that students' scientific explanations can reveal particular challenges with understanding key science concepts. In the case of Josh and Sarah, they appear to have an accurate understanding of the science concepts, but do not describe them in depth. Later in this chapter, we will return to the food web and chemical reaction cases from Chapter 5 and provide examples that illustrate student difficulties with the key science ideas. The final aspect focuses on the holistic quality of the scientific explanation. The components of the framework provide a guide to what students should include in their scientific explanations, but they should not become an algorithm or fill in the blank as part of their writing. The framework should be used to support or justify a claim and the scientific explanation should read as a coherent paragraph. If the holistic quality of the scientific explanation is weak, this can be an important area to comment on or provide questions around as well. We will provide more examples of types of feedback as we discuss the student examples from the fifth and seventh grade classrooms.

Students' scientific explanations can be used in a variety of ways as an assessment. You can use them as both summative and formative assessments and diagnostic tools to encourage student reflection, modify your own instruction based on students' strengths and weaknesses, provide students with specific and descriptive feedback, and evaluate end-of-unit or school-year student performance. Using assessments in this manner will support all your students to develop an understanding of science content and important twenty-first-century skills of written communication and the use of evidence.

Using Rubrics to Support Student Learning

Rubrics can be an essential tool to diagnose the strengths and weaknesses of student writing as well as provide information to inform future instruction and to provide students with specific and descriptive feedback. As we discussed in Chapter 5, when developing rubrics for scientific explanation tasks, we combine the framework (i.e., claim, evidence, reasoning, and rebuttal) with the science content to develop specific rubrics for each learning and assessment task. Consequently, using the rubrics to evaluate student work can provide insight both into students' understanding of scientific explanation and their understanding of the science content. In this section, we illustrate this process using work from fifth- and seventh-grade students for the two science assessment items developed in the food web and chemical reaction cases in Chapter 5. We describe how the rubrics can be used to analyze student work as well as how that analysis can be used to inform and modify future instruction and to provide students with specific and descriptive feedback.

Fifth-grade Food Web Case

As we discussed in Chapter 5, Mr. Cardone developed a food web assessment item to include in the end-of-year assessment of his fifth-grade students. Mr. Cardone taught in a large urban district in an elementary school with an ethnically diverse population of students. The majority of the students in Mr. Cardone's class were English language learners (ELLs) and many of them struggled with science writing at the beginning of the school year. He developed this item because food webs were a key concept in his fifth-grade curriculum, and because throughout the year he had been integrating strategies to support his students in constructing scientific arguments in which they justified their claim with appropriate evidence and reasoning. The food web assessment item asked his students to examine a food web and then to: *Write a scientific argument that answers the following question: What would happen to the size of the hawk population if all of the seeds were removed from the ecosystem? Remember to support your claim with evidence and reasoning* (see Figure 5.3 for the item).

Strong Fifth-grade Example. Mr. Cardone knew that some aspects of the framework were still challenging for his students. His goal was for his students to construct the appropriate claim (e.g., the hawk population would decrease) and support that claim with evidence and a little bit of reasoning. Figure 6.1 is one of the stronger examples of student writing from his two fifth-grade classrooms that illustrates the achievement of this goal. In this example, Dianne receives the highest score of a 2 for her claim (see Table 5.6 for rubric), because she begins with the appropriate and complete claim: "The hawk population would decrease."

In terms of evidence, the rubric includes four different components that the students should discuss—describing what the hawk, squirrel, sparrow, and rabbit

---

FIGURE 6.1

Strong Fifth-grade Example

The Hawk population would decrease because the Hawk eats two things squirrels & sparrows both of those animals eat seeds. First the squirrels would die which would mean one less food for the Hawk. The Sparrow population would decrease, which means less food for the hawk. That means the Hawk population will decrease.

128

Using
Rubrics and
Student Data
to Inform
Instruction

eat in the food web in relation to their population size. In her scientific argument, Dianne discusses what three of the organisms eat—hawk, squirrel, and sparrow— but does not discuss the rabbit as another food source for the hawk or that the size of the rabbit population would stay the same, because the rabbit does not eat seeds. Consequently, Dianne's evidence score is between a 2 and 3 because she completely discusses the role of the squirrel and the sparrow, but does not mention the rabbit or that hawks eat rabbits. This example illustrates that even with a detailed rubric there are still shades of gray in terms of scoring, because there are different ways to interpret or score a student response. Depending on the age and experience of your students, you would need to decide on how strictly to use the rubric and whether to give this sample of writing a 2 or a 3 or perhaps a score of 2.5 to illustrate the writing is between levels in terms of the quality of evidence provided. In terms of feedback, a specific comment or question about the role of the rabbit would help Dianne think about this organism in the food web; for example: *You include strong evidence in terms of the squirrel and sparrow. What evidence could you include about how the rabbit population impacts the population size of the hawk?*

Finally, in terms of reasoning, Dianne receives a level 1 out of 2. At the end of her scientific argument, she writes that there is "less food for the hawk. That means the hawk population will decrease," which explains why changing the population size of sparrow and squirrel will impact the hawk. She does not include in her reasoning a statement summarizing the general science principle that she is applying: *Organisms are affected by other organisms in a food web even if they are not directly linked to them.* Including this type of general science principle can be challenging for younger or less-experienced students. This characteristic of including general science principles in scientific explanations should become more prevalent as students have more experience supporting their claims with evidence and reasoning. Here again you could push Dianne's reasoning by providing specific feedback to encourage her to think about this aspect: *What understanding of food webs did you use to understand this diagram? In your reasoning, you should explicitly state the science concept that you applied—organisms are affected by other plants and animals in a food web even if they do not directly eat them.* In this case, besides providing questions a specific example of what the reasoning could look like can help students understand what is missing from their scientific argument. The idea of including a "scientific concept" is too abstract for students to conceptualize without a concrete example of what this might look like. Overall, Dianne does appropriately justify her claim with evidence and reasoning though she has room to grow as she continues on to middle school.

Fifth-grade Example with Incomplete Justification. The next example from Mr. Cardone's fifth-grade students illustrates a challenge that a number of his students had in writing their scientific arguments. For this food web assessment item, the majority of his students were able to construct the correct claim and

FIGURE 6.2

Fifth-grade Example with Incomplete Justification

The squirrel will die because it has no seeds to eat. and the Population of the Hawks will decrease.

provide some evidence to support that claim. Yet most of the students' evidence was incomplete and they did not include any reasoning for why their evidence supported their claim. For example, in Figure 6.2, Rosalia receives the highest level of a 2 for her claim because she does have the correct claim that "the population of the hawks will decrease." In terms of evidence, she receives a level 1 out of 4 because she includes one piece of evidence that "the squirrel will die because it has no seeds to eat." Consequently, she includes some evidence for her claim, but it is incomplete because she does not talk about what would happen to the populations of sparrow and rabbit. She also does not explicitly state what the hawk eats. Feedback for Rosalia in terms of evidence might include a statement like: *You did a great job including one piece of evidence about the squirrel. What other evidence could you use? How do the population sizes of the sparrow and rabbit affect the hawk?*

Finally, in terms of reasoning, Rosalia receives a 0 out of 2 because she does not include any reasoning in her argument. She does not explain why the squirrel dying would affect the population size of the hawk. For reasoning, the feedback could specifically address this concern: *Why does the squirrel dying let you know that the hawk population will decrease? Why is this piece of evidence important for your claim?* The feedback pushes Rosalia to think more deeply and more systematically about her evidence and reasoning. Rosalia's example provides a good illustration of using a scientific explanation to diagnose a student's weakness and using that diagnosis to provide feedback to support student learning.

Fifth-grade Example with No Claim. The student examples and video in this book come from the first year that Mr. Cardone used the claim, evidence, and reasoning framework with his students. At the beginning of the school year, when Mr. Cardone examined the first piece of writing in which he asked his students to

130

Using
Rubrics and
Student Data
to Inform
Instruction

FIGURE 6.3

Fifth-grade Example with No Claim

The squirrel would die & the sparrow would stay alive because it could still eat the grass hopper, the Halk would still have food

write a scientific argument he was surprised that so many of his fifth-grade students struggled to write a claim that addressed the question. Instead, their writing was descriptive and focused on the general science topic or consisted of a personal narrative or story. Consequently, throughout the school year he focused on helping his students see the importance of writing a claim that answered the question. In examining the food web assessment items from the end of the year, he was pleased to find that only two students across both of his fifth-grade classrooms did not construct a claim that specifically answered the question in the assessment item. This was a vast improvement from the beginning of the year. Figure 6.3 illustrates one of the examples of a student who did not construct a claim.

This example comes from Eduardo who recently moved to the United States from Colombia and spoke Spanish at home with his family. Because Eduardo struggled with his science writing, Mr. Cardone felt it was particularly important to provide him with specific feedback on both the positive aspects of his writing and the areas that needed improvement. Providing regular and specific feedback to English language learners in terms of both the strengths of their work and areas that need improvement is essential for supporting student learning of both content and language skills (Echevarria, Vogt, & Short, 2008). In terms of his claim, the only statement Eduardo makes about the hawk is that "the hawk would still have food." He does not state whether the population size of the hawk would change. Consequently, Eduardo receives a 0 out of 2 for his claim. In providing him with feedback, it is important to really focus him on what the question is asking. Feedback could include circling or highlighting the part of the question that says, "What would happen to the size of the hawk population," as well as provide specific suggestions for improvement: *You are correct that the hawk would still have food! Would the hawk have the same amount of food or less food? How would this impact the population size of the hawk—would the population be the same or smaller?*

In terms of evidence, Eduardo does correctly interpret two pieces of data from the food web that the squirrel would die (because it does not have seeds) and the sparrow would stay alive because it will still eat the grasshopper. Consequently, this sample of student writing received a level 2 out of 4 for evidence. He also receives a Level 0 out of 2 for reasoning, because he did not include any in his argument. In order to help Eduardo improve his evidence as well as encourage him to include reasoning in his writing, specific feedback could focus on these two aspects: *You did a great job in your response providing evidence about both the squirrel and sparrow. What other evidence could you include about the rabbit? What does all this evidence tell you in terms of what will happen to the population size of the hawk?* Specific and descriptive feedback can help all students, including English language learners, move forward toward constructing stronger claims and justifications for those claims in science.

Fifth-grade Example with an Inappropriate Claim. The last example from Mr. Cardone's class illustrates a student who struggled with a key science concept around food webs. The majority of the fifth-grade students in Mr. Cardone's two classes were able to correctly interpret the food web and understand that even though the hawk did not eat seeds, the hawk's population size would still be impacted, because the hawk ate other organisms (e.g., squirrels and sparrows) that ate seeds. Consequently, at the end of the school year Mr. Cardone's students did not seem to have the common alternative conception that "if the population size of one organism in a food web changes, it will only impact other organisms that are directly linked to that organism." (See Table 5.2.) Mr. Cardone was pleased that the majority of his students correctly understood the indirect relationships in the food web.

Interestingly, a couple of his students appeared to have a different alternative conception in their response to this assessment item. Figure 6.4 illustrates this difficulty. In this example, Pedro writes the wrong claim: "The Hawk population will not really change." Consequently, he receives a 0 for his claim out of a possible 2 levels. Pedro then continues in his writing to provide some correct data from the food web describing that the hawk will "lose one animal the squirrel" because "the squirrel eats the seed," but that there will still be some sparrows for the hawk to eat because "the sparrow eat the seed to but the sparrow can eat the grasshopper." Consequently, he does discuss two correct pieces of data from the food web and receives a level 2 for evidence.

Pedro's real challenge appears to be with the science principle and his reasoning. His writing suggests that he thinks as long as the hawk has something to eat that the population size of the hawk will not change: " . . . so that mean the hawk only loses one animal the squirrel. The reason I said that was because if you see my data you see that nothing will change in the detal." He does not seem to understand that by taking away the seeds there will be no squirrels and fewer sparrows so there will be less overall for the hawk to eat so the population size of the hawk will decrease.

If this assessment item had just been a multiple-choice item and Pedro had not included a justification for his claim, Mr. Cardone may incorrectly assume that he

132

Using
Rubrics and
Student Data
to Inform
Instruction

FIGURE 6.4

Fifth-grade Example with Inappropriate Claim

> The Hawk population will not really change.
> The evidence I have to poure this is that the
> Squirrel eats the seed and that the sparrow eat
> the seed to but the sparrow can eat the
> grasshopper to so that mean the hawk only
> loses one amimal the squirrel. The reason I
> said that was because, if you see my
> data you will see that nothing will
> change in the data

did not have any understanding of indirect relationships. Pedro does understand that removing the seeds will result in the squirrels dying out and that the hawk eats the squirrels. Yet Pedro's understanding is incomplete for he does not seem to understand how the loss of the squirrels will impact the hawk population size. Multiple-choice items frequently just focus on the claim. As these examples illustrate, a student can come up with a correct claim, but still not have a complete understanding of the science ideas or they can come up with the incorrect claim and still have some conceptual understanding. Writing scientific explanations, compared to just answering a multiple-choice item, can make students' thinking visible and provide the teacher greater insights into student understandings.

Pedro's example provides an excellent example of using scientific explanation as a diagnostic tool. In this case, it may be more important to focus the feedback on the science content, rather than on the structure of the claim, evidence and reasoning. For example, the feedback might say: *You are correct that there will be no more squirrels! There will also be fewer sparrows, because they will have less to eat. With no squirrels and fewer sparrows, do you think the size of the hawk population will stay the same? If there is less food available for the hawks, will all of the hawks live or will some of them no longer be able to get food?* This type of feedback can help students revisit their understanding of the science content. Discovering this type of confusion in the students' understanding of the science content can also inform the modification of future instruction to help the students better understand these ideas.

Plans to Modify Future Instruction. Because this was the first year Mr. Cardone used the claim, evidence, and reasoning framework with his students, he learned much from the experience that he plans to utilize in the next school year. Overall, he was pleased with his students' writing on the end-of-year food web assessment, because the majority of them were able to provide the correct claim and justify that claim with some evidence. Yet he already has ideas for how he would like to change his instruction. He learned at the beginning of the year that his students had difficulty constructing claims, as illustrated in Figure 6.3, and at the end of the year, although they were better able to construct claims and use evidence, that he would like to see more evidence and reasoning in their writing. Over the course of the school year, he designed strategies that worked well for his students based on examining earlier samples of student work, but these strategies were not integrated into his classroom instruction until later in the school year. In the subsequent year, he plans to utilize some of these strategies starting from the first week of school. Specifically, his students benefited from curricular scaffolds that broke down the learning task into claim, evidence, and reasoning as well as provided content-specific prompts about what to include for each component (see Figure 3.3). Furthermore, he found that using a student sheet providing different choices for the claim, evidence, and reasoning (see Figure 4.6) and then debating those choices as a class (see video clip 4.11) helped his students develop a stronger understanding of what counts as appropriate claim, evidence, and reasoning in science. By using some of these strategies earlier in the year, he hopes that his future students will be able to demonstrate even higher levels of sophistication in their writing by the end of the school year.

Seventh-grade Chemical Reaction Case

As we discussed in Chapter 5, the chemical reaction assessment item was designed for a final unit test for an 8-week chemistry unit for seventh-grade students. The four student writing examples in this chapter all come from Ms. Getty's classroom. Ms. Getty taught in a large urban district in a public K-8 school with an ethnically diverse population of students. Ms. Getty had been using the claim, evidence, and reasoning strategy in her seventh-grade science classroom for a couple of years and had incorporated a variety of teaching strategies into her lessons, including the use of everyday examples as illustrated in video clip 4.4. The chemical reaction assessment item required her students to analyze the data table to answer the following: *Write a **scientific explanation** that states whether a chemical reaction occurred when Carlos stirred and heated butanic acid and butanol* (see Figure 5.4 for the item).

Strong Seventh-grade Example. Ms. Getty's students developed a strong understanding of the claim, evidence, and reasoning framework and the majority of the students were able to successfully write the correct claim and justify the claim with both evidence and reasoning. Figure 6.5 is an example of one student,

134

Using
Rubrics and
Student Data
to Inform
Instruction

FIGURE 6.5

Strong Seventh-grade Example

A chemical reaction did occur in this
experiment. In a chemical reaction takes
place something new is made. When something
new is made properties change. If just
1 property changes then a chemical
reaction occured and a new substance was
made. In the experiment properties changed.
The melting points went from -7.9°C and
-89.5°C to -91.5°C and 0.0°C. Both of
the densitie also changed from 0.969/cm³ and 0.81g/cm³
to 0.87g/cm³ and 1.00g/cm³. Also 1 of the new
substances in now not soluable in water when
Page 3 before both were. Therefore, a chemical reaction Go to next page
did occur, because new substances were made and
properties changed.

Jose, who wrote a strong scientific explanation. For the claim, he received the
highest possible score of 1 for the claim (see Table 5.7 for the rubric), because
he correctly states, "A chemical reaction did occur in this experiment." He also
receives the highest score of a 3 for evidence, because he correctly describes how
the solubilities, melting points, and densities changed from before stirring and
heating compared to after stirring and heating. Finally, his reasoning is also strong
and he receives a level 2 out of 3 for describing the scientific principle he used to
make sense of the data table and construct his claim. Jose's reasoning states, "In
a chemical reaction takes place something new is made. When something new
is made properties change. If just 1 property changes then a chemical reaction
occurred and a new substance was made." He also returns to his reasoning after
describing his evidence by stating at the end, "Therefore, a chemical reaction did
occur because new substances were made and properties changed." In his reasoning,
he includes two components from the rubric: (1) a chemical reaction creates new or
different substances, and (2) different substances have different properties. The only
component he did not discuss was why he used solubility, density, and melting point
as evidence, but not the volume. He did not describe how three of the measurements
are properties while volume is not a property of a substance because it is not

independent of the sample size. Feedback on this item could include a question specifically encouraging Jose to talk about why he did not use volume: *You did an excellent job supporting your claim with evidence and reasoning! The one thing I would have liked you to talk more about in your reasoning is why you decided not to use volume as evidence. (This is correct!) Why is volume not good evidence to decide if a chemical reaction occurred?*

Similar to the food web example, the level of detail in the rubric and strictness that you use to follow the rubric will depend on the age and experience of your students. This example illustrates how the seventh-grade students were able to more easily include general scientific principles in their reasoning to support the claims they are making compared to the fifth-grade students. Jose does an excellent job describing what a chemical reaction is and how he knew a chemical reaction took place based on the data that was provided in the assessment item. With support, grade 5–8 students can achieve greater success at scientific explanations over time.

Seventh-grade Example with Incomplete Justification. The majority of Ms. Getty's students did justify their claims with evidence and reasoning. Yet similar to the fifth-grade examples, some students still struggled with including enough evidence or any reasoning. This is not surprising as writing in this fashion is challenging for learners and takes many years with thoughtful instruction and feedback in order for students to develop. Figure 6.6 illustrates a seventh-grade student, Dana, who provides the correct claim, but only provides one piece of evidence and no reasoning to support her claim. Dana's scientific explanation receives the highest score of 1 for claim, because she states, "A chemical reaction did occured in this experiment." She then receives a 1 out of 3 for evidence, because she states, "The melting points had changed." Since she does not discuss the other data (i.e., solubility and density), potential feedback for evidence could state: *Changing*

FIGURE 6.6

Seventh-grade Example with Incomplete Justification

A chimical recationdid occured in this experiment. Thereason for that is the butanicacid and butanol recacted witheach oter. The melting points hadchanced. Therecor a chemical reaction acured.

136

Using
Rubrics and
Student Data
to Inform
Instruction

*melting points is great evidence that a chemical reaction has occurred. What other
two pieces of evidence could you use to better support your claim?*

In terms of reasoning, Dana's scientific explanation receives a 0 out of 3,
because she does not describe why a change in melting point allows her to know
that a chemical reaction occurred. She does not discuss that new properties mean
that there is a new substance or that a chemical reaction creates a new substance.
Potential feedback for Dana could include: *Why does a change in melting point tell
you that a chemical reaction occurred? What happens during a chemical reaction?*
Even older middle school students can struggle with providing appropriate evidence
and reasoning for their claims. It may not be clear to them what counts as evidence
or reasoning in a particular content area or for a specific assessment item. Using the
specific scientific explanation rubric helps diagnose these challenges in order to provide more targeted feedback to students to support them in improving their writing.

Seventh-grade Example with Inappropriate Evidence. The next example,
in Figure 6.7, is from a student, Carmen, who struggled with what counted as
appropriate evidence for this specific assessment item. For Carmen's scientific
explanation, she receives a level 1 out of 1 for her claim, "Yes, a chemical reaction
did occur." Furthermore, her reasoning expresses a partially correct understanding
of the science in that she states, "A chemical reaction occurd because some of the
properties are different." She appears to understand that she wants to look at whether
the properties are different to determine whether a chemical reaction occurred. Yet
her evidence incorrectly compares the density of sample A and sample B, which are
the two layers after heating and stirring. In order to determine whether a chemical
reaction occurred, she needs to compare the density of the two liquids before

FIGURE 6.7
Seventh-grade Example with Inappropriate Evidence

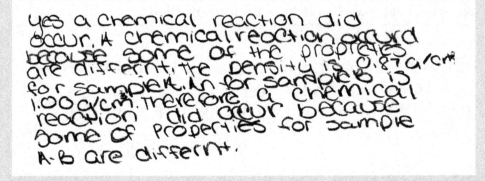

heating and stirring (i.e., butanic acid and butanol) to the density of the two liquids after heating and stirring (i.e., layer A and layer B). Consequently, Carmen receives a 0 for evidence, because she makes the wrong comparison.

Her reasoning could either receive a level 0 or a level 1 depending on how strictly you want to code her based on her comparison of the incorrect pairs. She knows that it is important to look at properties for differences, but she is confused about what properties to compare. Similar to the food web examples we discussed, your decision on how to use the rubric depends on the age and experience of your students. We would give the student the higher score, in this case providing Carmen with a 1 for reasoning, in order to acknowledge the strengths in her scientific explanation. The feedback could encourage her to think about what data to compare in order to answer this question: *You are correct that it is important to examine whether properties are different to determine if a chemical reaction occurred! What properties should you look at? Do you want to look at the properties of the substances after mixing or do you want to compare the properties of the substances before (butanic acid and butanol) to the properties of the substances after mixing (layers A and B)? What evidence should you use to support your claim that a chemical reaction occurred?* This feedback focuses more on the science concept in terms of how you determine whether a chemical reaction occurred rather than the structure of claim, evidence, and reasoning and has the potential to engage Carmen in thinking about the content. Carmen's response includes the correct structure; her difficulty is in understanding the science in terms of what counts as correct evidence for her claim.

Seventh-grade Example with Inappropriate Claim. The last example, in Figure 6.8, illustrates another student, Chris, who appeared to struggle with the science content. Chris's scientific explanation receives a 0 for the claim, because he makes the incorrect claim, "A chemical reaction didn't occure when Carlos stirred and heated butanic acid and butant." He then goes on to provide some interesting reasoning in that he writes, "In a CR the property should change and something should be made new but in this nothing was mad new. Therefore, this is not a CR."

FIGURE 6.8
Seventh-grade Example with Inappropriate Claim

A chemical reaction didn't occure when Carlos stirred and heated butanic acid and butant. In a CR. the property should change and, something should be made new but in this nothing was mad new. therefore, this is not a CR.

138

Using
Rubrics and
Student Data
to Inform
Instruction

In terms of reasoning, Chris's explanation could receive a level 1 or level 0, because he does appear to understand that in a chemical reaction the properties change. Similar to the other examples, the strictness of the use of the rubric can vary, though in our own scoring we did give the explanation a level 1 for reasoning. Although Chris understands he is looking for a change in properties and something new, he concludes a chemical reaction did not occur. Unfortunately, he did not provide any evidence so it is not clear what data he used to come to that particular claim. One common alternative conception that students have is they struggle with what characteristics count as properties that can be used to differentiate substances (see Table 5.3), which might be what is confusing Chris in this case. Another potential challenge is that Chris struggled to interpret the data table. Since the exact confusion is unclear, probing questions would be important feedback: *Why do you think nothing new was formed? How do properties provide evidence of whether or not a chemical reaction occurred? What properties were different before and after stirring and heating?*

Although the exact cause of Chris's confusion is unclear, the written explanation still provides greater insight into student thinking compared to if he had circled a multiple-choice item that a chemical reaction did not occur. By having students articulate the justification for their claims, students' thinking is made visible that can help you as the teacher diagnose student challenges and provide feedback to encourage student reflection as well as to inform future instruction.

Plans to Modify Future Instruction. The majority of Ms. Getty's seventh-grade students were able to construct the correct claim that a chemical reaction occurred as well as provide some evidence and reasoning to support that claim. Across her six different classes of seventh-grade students, there were relatively few students who struggled with this chemical reaction assessment item. The three weaker examples included here illustrate that even the students who struggled still appear to have the basic structure of claim, evidence, and reasoning in their writing. Some students, such as Dana's example in Figure 6.6, struggled with including a sufficient or complete justification. Other students, such as Carmen in Figure 6.7 and Chris in Figure 6.8, appeared to struggle more with the chemical reaction content. Consequently, Ms. Getty does not necessarily have plans to change the teaching strategies she uses in her classroom around claim, evidence, and reasoning. Rather, she will continue to use the variety of strategies she has developed over the past couple of years and provide her students multiple opportunities to practice their science writing across a variety of content areas to help them develop a stronger understanding of what counts as appropriate evidence and reasoning in different contexts. She will also continue to provide specific feedback to students who struggle. By using a variety of classroom level strategies and feedback based on individual student responses, Ms. Getty will be able to support all her students in learning science content and writing scientific explanations.

Throughout the chapter, we describe potential feedback that could be provided for the eight different student examples to support them in developing a stronger understanding of both scientific explanation and the science content. We also want to illustrate what feedback looks like using an actual example of a teacher's written feedback provided to a student from Ms. Nelson's class.

Ms. Nelson had used the claim, evidence, and reasoning framework for a couple of years with her students and had incorporated multiple strategies into her teaching throughout the year, such as discussing the framework, as illustrated in video clip 2.1, and having students engage in peer critique, as illustrated in video clip 4.10. Besides having her students provide each other with feedback, Ms. Nelson also frequently wrote comments on students' work providing them with specific feedback on what to improve as well as models of her expectations in terms of the different components of the scientific explanation. Figure 6.9 is the scientific explanation from a student in Ms. Nelson's class, David. David wrote his scientific explanation after completing an experiment in which he investigated whether combining water and powdered drink mix was a chemical reaction. Before combining the water and drink mix, David recorded the color and density for the water and observations of the drink mix. David and his partner then combined the two in a flask. They boiled the mixture and collected the vapor in a second flask where it condensed into a liquid. The contents of the first flask were dried on a filter paper. David then determined the color and density of the liquid in the second flask as well as recorded observations of the dried powder on the filter paper. Ms. Nelson's expectation was that her students would use their data to write a scientific explanation, such as the following:

> *A chemical reaction did not occur (CLAIM). The color and density of the two liquids were the same before and after the experiment. Before the experiment, the water was clear and the density was 1.0 g/mL. After the experiment, the liquid was clear and the density was 1.0 g/mL (EVIDENCE). Since the properties were the same before and after the experiment, a new substance was not created. Since there is no new substance, a chemical reaction did not occur (REASONING).*

In David's case, his scientific explanation lacked specific details in his claim, evidence, and reasoning. His actual writing and Ms. Nelson's comments are in Figure 6.9. The larger print text is David's writing. David wrote:

Claim: *It's not.*

Evidence: *Because the water moved to the other flask and not the Kool-Aid.*

Reasoning: *Because my data is correct and I did my homework, which makes it double correct.*

140

Using
Rubrics and
Student Data
to Inform
Instruction

FIGURE 6.9

Feedback on Seventh-grade Scientific Explanation—Mixtures

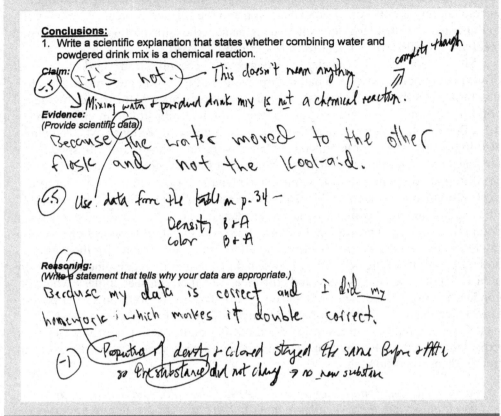

Ms. Nelson wanted David to include a more specific claim with a complete thought. She circled the claim and wrote next to it, "This doesn't mean anything." She then provided David with an example to illustrate what she was looking for in the claim: "Mixing water & powdered drink mix <u>is not</u> a chemical reaction." Ms. Nelson encouraged her students to write their claims in complete sentences and to avoid the use of vague pronouns.

For the evidence, Ms. Nelson circled the word *data* in the writing prompt and provided specific suggestions on what the data should look like: "Use data from the table on p. 34—Density B & A. Color B & A." She told David that he should be using the density and color from before and after the experiment. She wanted him to include specific observations and measurements from his experiment as evidence to support his claim. Finally, for the reasoning, David does not provide a rationale for why his evidence supports his claim and he does not include any scientific principles. Ms. Nelson provided an example to illustrate her expectations for reasoning: "Properties of density and color stayed the same before & after so the substance did not change → no new substance." Instead of just stating that "because my data is correct," she wanted him to include a justification that includes the key science concepts relevant to this question.

Ms. Nelson provided very detailed and specific feedback to help her students understand her expectations so that they would be able to meet those expectations when writing future scientific explanations. She often used examples to illustrate the type of writing students should include in their scientific explanations. She used a variety of teaching strategies, including written feedback on students' assignments, to help her students write specific claims and support those claims with appropriate evidence and reasoning. Although it took time for Ms. Nelson to provide such detailed feedback, it allowed her to provide individual support to each of her students ensuring that all her students learned how to write appropriate scientific explanations.

As we previously discussed, feedback can focus on the structure of the scientific explanation, the understanding of the science content or the holistic quality of the scientific explanation, depending on the particular difficulties of your students. In all three cases, the feedback should be specific and descriptive, providing comments on the strengths of the writing as well as suggestions on how to improve the writing. Providing student feedback takes time, which is often limited in the teaching profession, but it also provides valuable individualized support enabling all students to achieve greater success.

Check Point

In this chapter, we provide examples of how using rubrics to analyze students' written scientific explanations can provide numerous benefits. Students' writing can provide insights into their thinking and help teachers diagnose student difficulties. Teachers can use this information in order to inform and modify their instruction within one school year as well as in preparing to teach future students. Furthermore, providing students with specific and descriptive feedback can encourage them to reflect on and improve their science writing to include more detailed claims that specifically address the question or problem as well as provide evidence, reasoning, and even rebuttals to support their claim. Because providing feedback is tailored to individual students, it can support all students in developing a stronger understanding of the science content and of how to write scientific explanations. Assessments should not just be an end-of-teaching cycle; rather, they play a complex role in teaching both in diagnosing student difficulty and in analyzing how to improve teaching. Analyzing your students' writing may result in revisiting other topics we discussed earlier in the book, such as how to introduce the framework to your

142

Using
Rubrics and
Student Data
to Inform
Instruction

students, designing learning tasks, developing curricular scaffolds, integrating teaching strategies into your classroom, and designing assessments. Teaching is a constant cycle of teaching, reflection, and modification. In the final chapter, we focus on how to better support your students in constructing scientific explanations over time.

Study Group Questions

1. Use a rubric for scientific explanations to analyze some of your students' writing. You may want to do this with a group of teachers and compare all your scores. What are the strengths and weaknesses of their writing? Are there any common patterns across your students?
2. Based on your analysis of the student writing, what feedback would you provide your students? What aspects would you encourage them to focus on in future writing?
3. Based on your analysis of the student writing, how would you modify your instruction in the future? Are there any changes you would make to future lessons? If you think forward to the next school year, are there any changes you would make to how you would introduce the framework to your students?

7

Supporting Learning Over Time

How can using the claim, evidence, and reasoning framework change your classroom culture over time? How can it impact both your students' science writing and science talk? How can you use the framework to support your students in developing greater science understanding as well as build connections across different content areas? Let's consider the following vignette from Ms. Rodriguez's seventh-grade classroom:

> Ms. Rodriguez's class had been learning about the diversity of life and species. She gave them data about four different types of zebras and asked them to answer the following question: How many different species of zebras do these four types represent? Use evidence and reasoning to support your claim. After the students worked in groups to answer the question, they came back together to discuss their ideas as a class.

Ms. Rodriguez: We have been examining data to answer the question: How many different species do you think the four types of zebra represent? What claim did you come up with and what evidence did you use to support that claim?

Lin: We decided that there were four different species of zebra. Our evidence is that all four zebras have different types of stripes and they live in different areas.

Jake: I agree with Lin's group. Our group came up with the same claim. Our evidence was the stripes, where they live, and also the size of the zebras. The four types of zebras are different sizes. Since they live in different places and have different traits that means they are different species.

Ms. Rodriguez: Did any groups come up with a different claim than Lin's and Jake's groups?

Eduardo: Our group decided there were only three different species of zebra.

Chloe: What was your evidence for there being three species?

Marisa (another member of Eduardo's group): We read that Grant's zebra and Grevy's zebra can have offspring together and that the offspring can reproduce.

Ms. Rodriguez: Why is that piece of evidence important for your claim?

Marisa: We thought that what determined whether something is a species is whether they can reproduce and have fertile offspring. So we decided to focus on reproduction.

Deion: So are the traits more important, or is whether they can reproduce more important to determine whether something is a different species?

Ms. Rodriguez: That is a great question. All of the groups did an excellent job using evidence to support their claims. But it sounds like how the different groups were defining a species impacted what evidence they used to determine and support their claim. The different groups had different reasoning. Traditionally, scientists have defined a species as all organisms that can mate or reproduce with one another and produce fertile offspring [writes definition on the board]. I would like each group to go back and look at its evidence and its claim, considering this definition of a species. Using this definition of species, would you change either your claim or evidence?

This vignette shows how the language of claim, evidence, and reasoning has become a part of the culture of Ms. Rodriguez's classroom. In sharing their ideas with the classroom, the students provide evidence to support their claims, ask each other for their evidence, and try to understand the justifications for the different claims being considered. Integrating this language into the classroom norms takes time and does not occur as a result of one week of instruction. Ms. Rodriguez's classroom illustrates what can happen when the scientific explanation framework is used over a long period of time. In this final chapter, we explore three different areas to consider for potential future steps to support learning over time. First, we discuss how to develop a classroom culture that prioritizes scientific explanation in both writing and science talk. Next, we consider the concept of a learning progression, which focuses on a sequence of successively more complex ways of thinking about a science practice or science content over time. Finally, we discuss how the framework can be connected to other content areas such as mathematics, English language arts, or social studies in order to support students in developing twenty-first-century skills that can be applied across content areas and in a variety of contexts. This chapter provides potential areas of focus as you continue to refine your own teaching and work collaboratively with your colleagues to better support students over time.

Developing a Classroom Culture

Throughout the book, we discussed a number of ways to integrate the scientific explanation framework into your classroom to support greater student learning, such as how to: introduce the scientific explanation framework to your students, identify appropriate opportunities in your existing curriculum, design learning tasks, incorporate different teaching strategies, design assessment tasks, and use rubrics and student data to inform your instruction. Utilizing these different strategies over time can support the development of a classroom culture that prioritizes the roles of evidence, explanation, and argumentation. Science is not simply the memorization of facts, but rather science is a way of knowing that includes writing, talking, debating ideas, doing, thinking, and reasoning (Michaels, Shouse, & Schweingruber, 2008). Integrating the scientific explanation framework into your science classroom can shift your classroom culture to focus more on science as a practice that includes constructing, justifying, and debating different scientific claims using appropriate evidence and reasoning. This can help students understand that science is not just about memorizing discrete facts, but also about viewing science as a practice that includes its own ways of talking and writing.

Scientific inquiry requires students to play an active role and engage in science talk (Duschl et al., 2007). Although much of this book has focused on science writing, we also highlight the important role of science talk using the framework. Creating a classroom culture around the framework where claim, evidence, and reasoning become a part of the norms of classroom talk supports students in producing stronger written scientific explanations (McNeill, 2009). There is a relationship between the types of discussions that occur in your classroom and the writing that your students produce. Both ways of communicating should support this overarching idea that claims in science are determined and justified using evidence and reasoning. The vignette from Ms. Rodriguez's classroom illustrates a discussion in which the framework has become a part of the norms of classroom talk. The class discusses two different potential claims (i.e., there are four species of zebra versus three species of zebra) using evidence and scientific principles to determine the strength of those claims. In looking back at the vignette, there are three features that are particularly important for supporting this type of discussion: (1) the role of the scientific explanation framework in the discussion, (2) the pattern of teacher and student talk, and (3) the types of teacher questions. These features can help support all your students in taking part in meaningful discussions in which evidence and reasoning are used to support claims.

The Role of the Scientific Explanation Framework

Ms. Rodriguez's classroom discussion illustrates how the constructs of claim, evidence, and reasoning can become a part of the norms in classroom discussions. The framework can be explicitly observed in that the words claim, evidence, and reasoning are used effectively in the discussion by the teacher and students. For example, Ms. Rodriguez begins the discussion by asking: *What claim did you come up with and what evidence did you use to support that claim?* This language frames the discussion for students to help them understand that in their responses she is expecting them to provide claims and justify those claims with evidence. In addition to the teacher, the students also use these words, particularly in terms of referring to what they used as evidence to support their claims. Furthermore, one student (Chloe) even asks another group: *What was your evidence for there being three species?* This suggests that the students feel comfortable and know how to use this language as part of their science talk. In addition to the specific words (i.e., claim, evidence, and reasoning), the structure of the students' responses follows the claim, evidence, and reasoning format. For example, in Jake's response he provides a claim (four species), includes evidence (the stripes, where they live, and the size) and finally even states his reasoning: *Since they live in different places and have different traits, that means they are different species.* Although Jake does not explicitly identify this last statement as his reasoning, he is articulating why he thinks his evidence supports his claim. Consequently, we see in Ms. Rodriguez's classroom how the scientific explanation framework has both explicitly and implicitly impacted the classroom discussion.

The Pattern of Teacher and Student Talk

In terms of the pattern of teacher and student talk, science discussions have been characterized traditionally by the initiate, respond, and evaluate (IRE) pattern of discourse (Lemke, 1990). During IRE, the discussion alternates between teacher, student, teacher, student and teacher in a hierarchical pattern that is always dominated by the teacher. The illustrative discussion in Ms. Rodriguez's classroom is not characterized by this pattern. Rather, the students respond to each other's ideas and try to build a class consensus in terms of the strongest claim to address the question of how many species of zebra the four types represent. If the discussion had followed the IRE pattern, it may have looked like the following:

Teacher: How many species of zebra do these four types represent?

Student 1: Four species.

Teacher: Ok. You are on the right track. Did anyone come up with a different answer?

Student 2: There are three species.

Teacher: Great. There are three types of species. How have we defined species?

Student 3: A species is all animals that can reproduce with each other and create offspring.

Teacher: Excellent. A species is defined as all organisms that can mate with one another and produce fertile offspring. That is why there are only three species here. Since two of these types of zebra can mate with each other, that means they are the same species and there are only three total species.

In this sample discussion, the teacher initiates a question (I), student 1 responds (R), the teacher evaluates the student response (E). Then the teacher asks another question (I), student 2 responds (R), and the teacher evaluates (E). The limitations of this discussion include that the teacher does not know why student 1 responded that there were four species or why student 2 responded that there were three species. Furthermore, the teacher does not know the ideas of the rest of the class outside of these three students or whether or not those ideas changed over the course of the discussion. The students' responses are short, do not explain their justifications, and do not connect or build on the ideas of their peers. Moreover, the students are not engaged in the type of talk that characterizes science and are not playing an active role in this discussion. Students need opportunities to engage in science talk in order to become skilled at this practice (Duschl et al., 2007). That is not to say that the IRE pattern should never occur in the science classroom. The pattern of talk depends on the goal of instruction. There are times in a science classroom when the IRE pattern plays an important role, such as when you want to review science concepts that you previously discussed. The IRE pattern becomes problematic when it is the only discussion pattern that occurs in the classroom and students do not have opportunities to engage in science talk in which they respond to, evaluate, and build on each other's ideas.

The Types of Teacher Questions

The types of questions a teacher asks is essential to support students in justifying their claims, promote student-to-student discussion, and encourage students to support or refute the ideas of their classmates (McNeill & Pimentel, 2010). For example, as we mentioned previously, the initial question Ms. Rodriguez used to begin the discussion—*What claim did you come up with and what evidence did you use to support that claim?*—makes clear her expectations for the discussion to her students. The question illustrates that the teacher does not want the students to just tell her how many different species they think the four zebras represent; rather, the students also need to provide evidence to support why they are coming up with that particular claim. This is a very different opening to the discussion than the IRE pattern which begins with: *How many species of zebra do these four types represent?* In the IRE case, the student can simply respond with "four species" without providing any justification for that response. Asking students specifically for their evidence and reasoning encourages students to justify their responses and make their thinking visible to the teacher and to others in the classroom. This provides greater insight into student thinking, their level of understanding of the science content, and whether they hold any misconceptions.

Using more open-ended questions can also increase student talk and encourage them to justify their responses. For example, Ms. Rodriguez asks Marisa: *Why is that piece of evidence important for your claim?* In this case, Ms. Rodriguez is not looking for a specific "correct" response; instead, she is trying to understand Marisa's thought processes behind why reproduction is important for determining how many species of zebra exist. Again, this is in contrast to the IRE discussion where the teacher does not ask either student 1 or 2 why they came up with three or four different species. The teacher in the IRE discussion does ask the class: *How have we defined species?* This is an example of a closed or known answer question in which the teacher is looking for a specific right answer. Known answer questions are the most frequent type of question used in science classrooms (Lemke, 1990). Known answer questions do have a specific and important role in science classrooms such as reviewing or clarifying students' understandings of key science concepts. In Ms. Rodriguez's discussion, we do not see known answer questions playing an integral role, because her goal is to support students in justifying their claims and to encourage them to listen to and build off each other's ideas. Known answer questions would not provide as much support for her overarching goal.

Although this is only a hypothetical example, Ms. Rodriguez, like all teachers, does not want her students to walk away with a scientifically inaccurate definition of species, like Jake's definition that different species "live in different places and have different traits." She wants her students to develop an in-depth and scientifically accurate understanding of the science concepts. But she did not feel that this initial discussion was the appropriate time to "correct" Jake's definition when he initially introduced it to the class. Rather, the point of this discussion was to elicit a number of students' ideas, which is why the more open questions and student-to-student interactions were an appropriate structure for this discussion. Furthermore, by encouraging students to listen to each other's ideas and justify their claims, Ms. Rodriguez hopes that a number of students (including Jake) will refine their understanding of the concept of species. If Jake is able to realize on his own the error in his thinking through the class discussion and revisit his initial claim and evidence with his group, this will enable him to develop a richer understanding of species than if Ms. Rodriguez corrected his idea right away.

Finally, a last unique characteristic illustrated in the scenario with Ms. Rodriguez is that she specifically links to the ideas of previous students. For example, she asks: *Did any groups come up with a different claim than Lin's and Jake's groups?* By making comparisons to other groups, she is encouraging students to listen to each other and respond to each other's ideas. These types of links help students understand the importance of connecting their ideas to those of their peers. The questions teachers ask impact the nature of discussion that occurs. When the goal is to engage in a discussion in which students justify their ideas and build off the ideas of their peers, using the scientific explanation framework can help support this goal.

Video Example—Developing a Classroom Culture

Video clip 7.1 from Ms. Nelson's classroom illustrates a classroom where claim, evidence, and reasoning have become a part of the classroom culture. The clip also shows how students in this class have learned to listen to and communicate with each other. In this video, Ms. Nelson has projected three different examples of scientific explanations as part of the *How can I make new stuff from old stuff?* curriculum (McNeill et al., 2004). She then asks her students to critique them in terms of the strength and weaknesses of each example. The structure of this discussion is different than the typical science classroom in that it exhibits the three features: (1) students use the scientific explanation framework as normal components of the discussion, (2) students listen to each other and respond to each other's ideas, and (3) the teacher uses questions to support this discussion. In this clip, Ms. Nelson's students play a major role in the direction of the discussion. Her students listen to each other's comments and directly provide each other with feedback and questions during

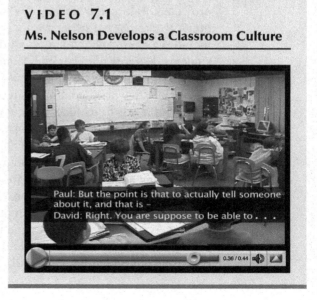

VIDEO 7.1

Ms. Nelson Develops a Classroom Culture

Paul: But the point is that to actually tell someone about it, and that is –
David: Right. You are suppose to be able to . . .

0.36 / 0.44

this whole class discussion. Below is an excerpt from Ms. Nelson's discussion that exhibits the features:

Ms. Nelson: Ok. Molly, what do you want to say?

Molly: I like number three.

James: It does not say anything about properties.

Molly: The last sentence says that—

Andrew: Yes, it talks about it.

Molly: —according to the—

Paul: It does not say the word though

Molly: —ones, the properties that we have gone over. Um, that they are different.

Ms. Nelson: Do you think it is ok that it does not have anything about properties? Specifically?

Molly: Yeah, because it has the names of them.

Paul: But, what if we do not know that they are properties?

[A couple of students talking at the same time.]

Paul: But the point is that to actually tell someone about it, and that is—

David: Right. You are suppose to be able to have some average Joe come up here and be able to understand what you are talking about.

Ms. Nelson begins the discussion by asking a very open question in order to support students in expressing their thinking about the three examples she has projected. Asking the student, "What do you want to say?" allows Molly the opportunity to express her ideas. Molly selects the third example as the strongest, which includes a claim and evidence, but does not include any reasoning. A number of students disagree with her choice and critique the third example, because of its lack of reasoning. Although the students do not explicitly say the term *reasoning* in this discussion, they are debating what counts as strong reasoning and whether or not the reasoning needs to include a discussion of properties. Paul's question, "But, what if we do not know that they are properties?" and David's comment, about "some average Joe," suggest that they understand the importance of explaining the evidence and why it supports the claim. Both students have fairly sophisticated understandings of what should be included in the reasoning. Throughout the discussion, the students regularly respond and provide feedback to each other. The students listen to each other and respond to each other's ideas. This type of peer support may help students become even stronger at engaging in scientific explanation, because they are regularly receiving support not only from the curriculum and from their teacher, but also from each other (McNeill, 2009).

Developing a classroom culture that incorporates the scientific explanation framework takes time, but it is essential to assist all students in learning science. Just as students need support in successfully writing a claim justified by evidence and reasoning, they need support knowing when to justify their claims during class discussions as well as questioning the claims of their peers. Yet when the framework becomes a part of the norms of classroom discussion it can help support student writing, and when it becomes part of the norms of student writing it can help support classroom discussions. Engaging in using evidence, constructing scientific explanations, and considering multiple alternative explanations are essential aspects of science that are not specific to either writing or talk. Rather, the scientific explanation framework supports science as a way of knowing that includes thinking, talking, writing, and reasoning. Over time as the framework becomes a part of your classroom, it will help students develop a stronger understanding of science as well as develop greater expertise in engaging in science.

A Learning Progression for Scientific Explanations

Because writing and discussing scientific explanations is a challenging task, it will take time to develop. One of the best ways for students to learn core aspects of science is to support students in learning more sophisticated ways of thinking about content or practices across multiple years (Michaels et al., 2008). A learning progression is a sequence of successively more complex ways of thinking about a science practice or science content that develop over time (Smith, Wiser, Anderson, & Krajcik, 2006). After you become comfortable using the scientific explanation framework in your classroom, you may want to then consider how to integrate the concept of a learning progression for scientific explanation across one school year or multiple school years in order to support your students in developing greater expertise.

As we discussed in previous chapters, the instructional framework for scientific explanation has multiple variations of different levels of complexity. Table 7.1 provides a summary of these different variations, which were also presented in Table 2.3. These multiple variations form a learning progression for scientific explanation.

The simplest version of the learning progression consists of claim, evidence, and reasoning with relatively simple definitions of each component. The evidence component becomes more complex in variation #2 as different characteristics of evidence are discussed such as the ideas of appropriateness and sufficiency of evidence. The reasoning component becomes more complex in variation #3 as each piece of evidence may require a different justification for why the evidence supports the claim. Finally, the most complex version of the learning progression also includes the idea of a rebuttal, which considers alternative explanations and

TABLE 7.1 Learning Progression for Scientific Explanation

Level of Complexity	Framework Sequence	Description of Framework for Students
Simple ↓ Complex	Variation #1 1. Claim 2. Evidence 3. Reasoning	Claim • a statement that answers the question Evidence • scientific data that supports the claim Reasoning • a justification for why the evidence supports the claim using scientific principles

	Variation #2
	1. Claim
	2. Evidence
	  • Appropriate
	  • Sufficient
	3. Reasoning
		Claim
		• a statement that answers the question
		Evidence
		• scientific data that supports the claim
		• data needs to be appropriate
		• data needs to be sufficient
		Reasoning
		• a justification for why the evidence supports the claim using scientific principles

	Variation #3
	1. Claim
	2. Evidence
	  • Appropriate
	  • Sufficient
	3. Reasoning
	  • Multiple components
		Claim
		• a statement that answers the question
		Evidence
		• scientific data that supports the claim
		• data needs to be appropriate
		• data needs to be sufficient
		Reasoning
		• a justification for why the evidence supports the claim using scientific principles
		• each piece of evidence may have a different justification for why it supports the claim

	Variation #4
	1. Claim
	2. Evidence
	  • Appropriate
	  • Sufficient
	3. Reasoning
	  • Multiple components
	4. Rebuttal
		Claim
		• a statement that answers the question
		Evidence
		• scientific data that supports the claim
		• data needs to be appropriate
		• data needs to be sufficient
		Reasoning
		• a justification for why the evidence supports the claim using scientific principles
		• each piece of evidence may have a different justification for why it supports the claim
		Rebuttal
		• describes alternative explanations, and provides counter evidence and reasoning for why the alternative explanation is not appropriate

provides counter evidence and reasoning for why the alternative is not appropriate. Each of the four variations increases in complexity and provides a pathway to increased sophistication. Over the course of a school year or with colleagues across many years, you can support students building more sophisticated ways of writing and discussing scientific explanations.

In terms of one school year, you may want to consider increasing the complexity of scientific explanations for your students as they develop greater expertise in this challenging scientific practice. For example, you could start just introducing the ideas of claim, evidence, and reasoning and over the course of the year present more complex ways of thinking about and using evidence by introducing the ideas of sufficient and appropriate evidence. If you teach students science across multiple years or work with other science teachers in your school or district, you may want to develop a plan for how to build student understanding of this practice across multiple grade levels. For example, you could move from variation #1 in fifth grade to variation #2 in sixth grade to variation #3 in seventh grade and finally to variation #4 in eighth grade. The learning progression should serve as a tool to support students in developing greater sophistication in their ability to construct and critique scientific explanations across time. Considering how scientific explanations are presented and discussed during each grade level can provide students with a more coherent science learning experience where each grade level builds on and supports what students learned the previous year. Supporting your students in building understandings across years will help ensure that students develop rich understandings of how to construct scientific explanations and will also help them develop important twenty-first-century skills such as communicating with others, critical thinking, and complex problem solving.

Connecting to Other Content Areas

The scientific explanation framework can support students in using reasoning and building understanding not only in science, but also in other content areas. Using evidence, constructing explanations, and critiquing other explanations are all twenty-first-century skills, which are important in many different contexts outside of the science classroom. As you become familiar with the framework, you may want to consider working with teachers in your school to connect claim, evidence, reasoning, and rebuttal to other content areas to help students make connections across their different classes, such as mathematics, science, social studies, and language arts. Making these connections can help students develop stronger critical thinking skills as they see how the practices and reasoning in each class connect to one another. Furthermore, this can also support students in developing stronger evidence-based writing and talk across the different content areas.

If you teach multiple content areas to your students, you can make these connections yourself across the disciplines for your students. Otherwise, you can talk to other teachers in your school to develop a common framework or connections across the content areas. For example, the teachers in a bilingual middle school decided that they wanted to use a common framework across language arts, science, mathematics, and social studies. They decided to adapt the CERR framework to instead be CERO: Claim, Evidence, Reasoning, and Other. *Other* stands for "other explanations and considerations," because the teachers felt that language was more applicable across the content areas than the term *rebuttal*. Furthermore, they preferred the acronym CERO, because cero means "zero" in Spanish. If students did not include CERO, they would receive a zero for their work. Table 7.2 displays how the language arts teacher used CERO in her classroom to support her students in developing persuasive writing.

Although the components are the same as the students use in their science class, the definitions for the language arts class focus specifically on how to write an argument supporting a claim using text. For example, while both science and language arts use evidence, in science the evidence focuses on scientific data such as observations and measurements while in language arts the evidence focuses on using quotes and other support from the text. Using the common language of evidence across the disciplines will help students learn that evidence is critical for supporting claims and that different fields have different criteria for what is accepted as evidence.

Another example comes from an elementary teacher, Ms. Reed, who taught all the subjects to her students during the school day. Ms. Reed was using claim,

---

TABLE 7.2 English Language Arts Example of CERO

	How to Answer an Open Response (*con CERO excepiones!*)
Claim	• Restate the question • Make a conclusion that answers the question being asked
Evidence	• Provide evidence from the text to support your claim • *Quote* the text directly • *Summarize* in your own words
Reasoning	• Connect the claim to the evidence • Explain why the textual support you chose really does prove your claim to be true[1]
Other	• Is there something else that will make your argument stronger? • Can you explain and refute a counterargument? • Can you end with a sense of closure, like a "fortune cookie"?

---

[1]In science, claims are neither true nor false; rather, they are supported or not supported by evidence and reasoning. As science develops, theories better explain and predict phenomena but they are not "true" while an old theory is false. In this example, the words are from the teacher in a language arts classroom and we did not want to change them.

TABLE 7.3 Mathematics Example of CER

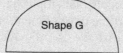

Shape G is not a triangle because it does not have an angle on top. And that's why it's not a triangle.

Evidence:
- No angle at top. The top is round.
- Only 2 angles
- Only 1 straight side

Reason:
A triangle must have 3 straight sides, not only 1. This is round; triangles have only straight sides.
A triangle must have 3 angles; this shape has two.

evidence, and reasoning in science and decided she also wanted her students to apply the framework in mathematics where the students were studying geometry. She gave each group of students a shape and asked them to write a CER to prove whether or not that shape was a triangle. Table 7.3 includes the response from one group of students. This example illustrates how students used evidence and reasoning to support their claim that Shape G was not a triangle. Similar to the language arts example, the components are the same as in science, but what counts as a claim, evidence, and reasoning is different for this mathematics example. In this example, the evidence focuses on the number of angles, the number of straight sides, and the number of round sides.

As you become comfortable with the scientific explanation framework, you may want to consider how to use the framework across content areas either in your own teaching or in work with other teachers. By using this common framework across the different content areas, you can talk to students about how people use evidence in different disciplines and different contexts. The use of evidence is prevalent in so many different situations, but exactly what that evidence looks like varies. Building the CER framework across different disciplines will help ensure your students develop and use this practice, not only in school but also in their daily lives.

Check Point

In the previous chapters, we discussed the importance of scientific explanations, a framework to introduce students to scientific explanation, steps to design learning tasks for your current science curriculum, teaching strategies to integrate into your classroom, steps to develop assessment tasks and rubrics, and ways to use rubrics and student data to inform instruction. In this chapter, we considered three different areas for potential future steps to support learning over time. First, developing a classroom culture with your students that emphasizes the role of scientific explanations takes time, but can support the development of norms in both classroom discussions and writing that prioritize the use of evidence and reasoning to support claims. After you become comfortable integrating the framework into your own classroom, you also may want to consider developing with your colleagues an instructional sequence for your school or school district using the learning progression presented in this chapter (see Table 7.1) to support students in developing more sophisticated understandings of scientific explanation over time. Finally, the CER framework is relevant not only to science, but also across other content areas and contexts. As part of your next steps, you might also want to consider how to connect it to other content areas to support your students in critical thinking, talking, and writing across the disciplines.

We hope this is only the beginning of your journey into integrating claims, evidence, and reasoning into your own teaching to better support your students' learning. Constructing scientific explanations is a complex practice that takes time to support, but it can also offer multiple rewards to both you and your students. As we emphasized throughout this book, all students are capable of taking part in this important practice. The more it is incorporated into your teaching and the more you support students, the deeper their understandings of this practice will grow. When students construct scientific explanations, they achieve greater success in science and build understanding of twenty-first-century skills of communication, critical thinking, and complex problem solving that they will be able to use throughout their lives.

Study Group Questions

1. Videotape or audiotape a classroom discussion in your science class that focuses on the scientific explanation framework. What was the role of the framework in the discussion? What was the pattern of teacher and student talk (e.g., IRE)? What type of questions did you ask? If you were going to teach the lesson again, what types of questions or other strategies could you use to better support your students?

2. Develop an instructional sequence for scientific explanation for your school or school district that builds off the learning progression in Table 7.1. How could you support students in constructing more complex scientific explanations across grade levels?

3. How similar and different is the CER framework from the types of writing and talk your students engage in for other classes (e.g., math, social studies, language arts)? How could you develop more connections with the other content areas to support your students in seeing how the framework can be used outside of science class?

References

American Association for the Advancement of Science. (1993). *Benchmarks for science literacy.* New York: Oxford University Press

American Association for the Advancement of Science. (2009). *Benchmarks Online.* Retrieved on January 25, 2010 – http://www.project2061.org/publications/bsl/online/index.php

Bell, P., & Linn, M. (2000). Scientific arguments as learning artifacts: Designing for learning from the web with KIE. *International Journal of Science Education, 22*(8), 797–817.

Berland, L. K., & Reiser, B. J. (2009). Making sense of argumentation and explanation. *Science Education, 93*(1), 26–55.

Black, P. (2003). The importance of everyday assessment. In J. M. Atkin & J. E. Coffey (Eds.), *Everyday assessment in the science classroom* (pp. 1–12). Arlington, VA: National Science Teachers Association Press.

Bransford, J., Brown, A., & Cocking, R. (Eds.). (2000). *How people learn: Brain, mind, experience and school.* Washington, DC: National Academy Press.

Council of Chief State School Officers and National Governors Association (2010). *Common Core State Standards for English Language Arts.* Retrieved on July 15, 2010 – http://www.corestandards.org/the-standards/english-language-arts-standards

Davies, A. (2003). Learning through assessment: Assessment for learning in the science classroom. In J. M. Atkin & J. E. Coffey (Eds.), *Everyday assessment in the science classroom* (pp. 13–26). Arlington, VA: National Science Teachers Association Press.

DeBoer, G. E. (2005). Standardizing test items. *Science Scope, 28*(4), 10–11.

Driver, R., Guesne, E., & Tiberghien, A. (Eds.). (1985). *Children's ideas in science.* Philadelphia: Open University Press.

Duschl, R. A., Schweingruber, H. A., & Shouse, A. W. (Eds.). (2007). *Taking science to school: Learning and teaching science in grades k-8.* Washington, DC: National Academy Press.

Echevarria, J., Vogt, M., & Short, D. S. (2008). *Making content comprehensible for English learners: The SIOP Model.* Boston, MA: Pearson, Allyn & Bacon.

Eilks, I., Moellering, J., & Valanides, N. (2007). Seventh-grade students' understanding of chemical reactions: Reflections from an action research interview study. *Eurasia journal of Mathematics, Science & Technology Education, 3(4)*, 271–286.

Erduran, S., Simon, S., & Osborne, J. (2004). TAPing into argumentation: Developments in the application of Toulmin's argument pattern for studying science discourse. *Science Education, 88(6)*, 915–933.

Gallegos, L., Jerezano, M. E., Flores, F. (1994). Preconceptions and relations used by children in the construction of food chains. *Journal of Research in Science Teaching, 31*: 259–272.

Hug, B., & McNeill, K. L. (2008). First and second hand experiences in science: Does data type influence classroom conversations? *International Journal of Science Education, 30(13)*, 1725–1751.

Jiménez-Aleixandre, M. P., Rodríguez, A. B., & Duschl, R. A. (2000). "Doing the lesson" or "doing science": argument in high school genetics. *Science Education, 84*, 757–792.

Krajcik, J., McNeill, K. L., & Reiser, B. (2008). Learning-goals-driven design model: Curriculum materials that align with national standards and incorporate project-based pedagogy. *Science Education, 92(1)*, 1–32.

Krajcik, J. S., & Sutherland, L. (2009). IQWST Materials: Meeting the Challenges of the 21st Century.

Lemke, J. (1990). *Talking science: Language, learning, and values.* Norwood, NJ: Ablex Publishing Corporation.

Maatta, D., Dobb, F., & Ostlund, K. (2006). Strategies for teaching science to English learners. In. A. K. Fatham & D. T. Crowther (Eds.), *Science for English language learners: K-12 classroom strategies* (pp. 37–59). Arlington, VA: National Science Teachers Association Press

McNeill, K. L. (2009). Teachers' use of curriculum to support students in writing scientific arguments to explain phenomena. *Science Education, 93(2)*, 233–268.

McNeill, K. L., Harris, C. J., Heitzman, M., Lizotte, D. J., Sutherland, L. M., & Krajcik, J. (2004). How can I make new stuff from old stuff? In J. Krajcik & B. J. Reiser (Eds.), *IQWST: Investigating and questioning our world through science and technology.* Ann Arbor, MI: University of Michigan.

McNeill, K. L., & Krajcik, J. (2007). Middle school students' use of appropriate and inappropriate evidence in writing scientific explanations. In M. Lovett & P. Shah (Eds.), *Thinking with data* (pp. 233–265). New York, NY: Taylor & Francis Group, LLC.

McNeill, K. L., & Krajcik, J. (2008a). Scientific explanations: Characterizing and evaluating the effects of teachers' instructional practices on student learning. *Journal of Research in Science Teaching, 45(1)*, 53–78.

McNeill, K. L., & Krajcik, J. (2008b). Assessing middle school students' content knowledge and reasoning through written scientific explanations. In J. Coffey, R. Douglas, & C. Stearns, (Eds.), *Assessing science learning: Perspectives from research and practice* (pp. 101–116). Arlington, VA: National Science Teachers Association Press.

McNeill, K. L., & Krajcik, J. (2009). Synergy between teacher practices and curricular scaffolds to support students in using domain specific and domain general knowledge in writing arguments to explain phenomena. *The Journal of the Learning Sciences,* 18(3), 416–460.

McNeill, K. L., Lizotte, D. J., Krajcik, J., & Marx, R. W. (2006). Supporting students' construction of scientific explanations by fading scaffolds in instructional materials. *The Journal of the Learning Sciences,* 15(2), 153–191.

McNeill, K. L., & Pimentel, D. S. (2010). Scientific discourse in three urban classrooms: The role of the teacher in engaging high school students in argumentation. *Science Education,* 94(2), 203–229.

Michaels, S., Shouse, A. W., & Schweingruber, H. A. (2008). *Ready, set, science! Putting research to work in k-8 science classrooms.* Board on Science Education, Center for Education, Division of Behavioral and Social Sciences and Education. Washington, DC: The National Academies Press.

Moje, E. B., Peek-Brown, D., Sutherland, L. M., Marx, R. W., Blumenfeld, P., & Krajcik, J. (2004). Explaining explanations: Developing scientific literacy in middle-school project-based science reforms. In D. Strickland & D. E. Alvermann (Eds.), *Bridging the gap: Improving literacy learning for preadolescent and adolescent learners in grades 4-12.* NY: Teachers College Press.

National Research Council. (1996). *National science education standards.* Washington, DC: National Academy Press.

National Research Council. (2000). *Inquiry and the national science education standards: A guide for teaching and learning.* Washington, DC: National Academy Press.

National Research Council. (2001). *Classroom assessment and the national science education standards.* Washington, DC: National Academy Press.

National Research Council. (2008). *Research on future skill demands: A workshop summary.* Washington, DC: National Academies Press.

Pellegrino, J. W., Chudowsky, N., & Glaser, R. (Eds.) (2001). *Knowing what students know: The science and design of educational assessment.* Washington, DC: National Academy Press.

Purcell-Gates, V., Duke, N. K., Martineau, J. A. (2007). Learning to read and write genre-specific text: Roles of authentic experience and explicit teaching. *Reading Research Quarterly,* 42(1), 8–45.

Rhoton, J., & Shane, P. (Eds.). (2006). *Teaching science in the 21st century.* Arlington, VA: National Science Teachers Association Press.

Rose, D. H., & Meyer, A. (2002). *Teaching every student in the Digital Age: Universal design for learning.* Alexandria, VA: ASCD.

Rosebery, A. S., & Hudicourt-Barnes, J. (2006). Using diversity as a strength in the science classroom: The benefits of science talk. In R. Douglas, M. P. Klentschy, K. Worth, & W. Binder (Eds.), *Linking science and literacy in the K–8 classroom* (pp. 305–319). Arlington, VA: National Science Teachers Association Press.

Smith, C. L., Wiser, M., Anderson, C. W., & Krajcik, J. (2006). Implications of research on children's learning for standards and assessment: A proposed learning progression for matter and the atomic molecular theory. *Measurement: Interdisciplinary Research and Perspectives,* 4(1&2), 1–98.

Sneider, C. I. (2003). Examining students' work. In J. M. Atkin & J. E. Coffey (Eds.), *Everyday assessment in the science classroom* (pp. 27–40). Arlington, VA: National Science Teachers Association Press.

Sutherland, L. M., McNeill, K. L., Krajcik, J., & Colson, K. (2006). Supporting students in developing scientific explanations. In R. Douglas, M. P. Klentschy, K. Worth, & W. Binder (Eds.), *Linking science and literacy in the K-8 classroom* (pp. 163–181). Arlington, VA: National Science Teachers Association Press.

Steele, M. (2005). Science Sampler: Teaching science to middle school students with learning problems. *Science Scope,* 29(2), 50–51.

Toulmin, S. (1958). *The uses of argument.* Cambridge, UK: Cambridge University Press.

Zohar, A., & Nemet, F. (2002). Fostering students' knowledge and argumentation skills through dilemmas in human genetics. *Journal of Research in Science Teaching*, 39(1), 35–62.

Index